DADDY'S STORY

EXPOSED

BABA DADDY

authorHOUSE®

AuthorHouse™ UK
1663 Liberty Drive
Bloomington, IN 47403 USA
www.authorhouse.co.uk
Phone: 0800.197.4150

Published by AuthorHouse   05/12/2015

ISBN: 978-1-5049-4148-8 (sc)
ISBN: 978-1-5049-4147-1 (hc)
ISBN: 978-1-5049-4149-5 (e)

I SEE YOUR TEARS

Written by Shazia.A

I see your tears,
But, not your fear
I know not why you cry
Still, by all means, you try,
To bring a smile on my face
Comforting me, you're my ace
And though, you struggle
Indeed, I am befuddled
You're growing weak, why away our happiness dwindled?
I have no sense,
Nothing I could comprehend, I am tensed
But, you stood forth, when I stumble
For I, you grew strong, yet though, you looked feeble
You smiled, along the way
Till I grew up, you had the magic wand like a fay
You made it, everything feasible
You're my daddy, you defend
Where it could be for me, an end
You opened the door, you held my hands
Together we walked, we shared
Together we're strong, we care
No one else could,
And I am the girl today
For your love enlightened my way
Now I see the lights, I hear the song, there's happiness
Only because you were there in my moments of sadness
And no tears should I ever let you shed
No other pain, no fret
But only your smile,
I need for the rest of my life

DADDY'S STORY

This story is dedicated to my daughter; I hope and pray that one day you will understand everything.

I want to begin this story for you by describing or mentioning just a few lines from a well known song. By luck maybe, I originally heard this song at the right time, it was a moment of my life where I was unsure about everything going on around me. This particular song is a song that I heard whilst I was going through the insane torture of the issues and troubles that I had to fight. I never set out to hear this song, to be honest I never took notice of it prior to this day, even though I knew of it, but I only knew the tune and not the words. That day I randomly heard it on the radio whilst I was driving home from work to an empty house as your mum had the privilege of having you that weekend and you were set to stay at your nanny's house. The song instantly hit home, every word I heard was exactly how I felt inside, it had anger, it had frustration, you could feel the agony within the words being sung, but also at the same time it was telling me I had a reason to be here. The song made sense that my story, my life that I was living had to be told, it was from that moment it became a motivational tool for me. Whilst I wrote this book I would frequently listen to this to help me see and understand my clear goal and target I had set myself, because believe me there was numerous times I thought you shouldn't have to hear our story, and many times where I just gave up on the whole idea.

There is no need for me to place the fact that a song meant something to me within this story, but I just want to begin the story with a few key lines from the song before I allow you to read on. I want you to see or try to understand that I am only human and that sometimes we take for granted who we are and what we are, and then there are those who don't care or feel for other people's emotions. So please understand I had to write this story for you, and maybe for the whole world to read and digest.

The song itself is a very well known song, as you will find out I refuse to name people within this book and although maybe I should highlight the song title and the artist I am going to stick to my guns and not do so, but I know your smart, and I know with all the tools we have at our disposal you will easily find all the details for the song if you ever wish to do so. Here are a few of the lines that meant so much, because it feels like every word was written for me by me.

"You've got the words to change a nation, but you're biting your tongue"

"You've spent a lifetime stuck in silence afraid you'll say something wrong"

"If no one ever hears it, how we gonna learn your song"

"You've got a heart as loud as lions so why let your voice be tamed"

"You've got the lights to fight the shadows so stop hiding it away"

"If the truth has been forbidden, then we're breaking all the rules"

"There's no need to be afraid"

"When did we all get so fearful?"

"I wanna shout, I wanna scream till the words dry out, so put it in all of the papers, I'm not afraid, they can read all about it"

So that's what I did, I've wrote you my story, and I don't care who reads it, I don't care if no one understands it, as long as you're the sole person who does, that's my goal. I never went through hell for them, only you.

EVERY STORY HAS AN INTRODUCTION

To my dear daughter, never did I once ever feel or think I'd ever need to express myself the way I am about to, never did I ever feel I'd ever write my own daughter a story like this, but no one will ever understand how I feel or understand the experiences I have been put through, except you.

I've always from a young age liked to write down my views, always liked to tell stories based on my life, so it's no surprise that it has come to this. I've always been like this because I feel no trust in any one, I ultimately feel I am alone in this world, battling my own wars but never winning. It hurts me to write you such a story that emotionally has drained every little bit of strength I have built up, a story which has knocked every ounce of confidence I have within me, a story which hand on heart, has brought me to my lowest in my whole life with no ending in sight. You need to understand this story is real, every word I write has happened. I know in time you will forget everything I have done for you, It also hurts me that you won't realise how strong I was for you, how I fought for you, how I tried to stop harm from ever getting near you, but your dad wants you to remember, and I want you to be proud of who you are, because I never went through all this alone, you lived through it as well, and that to me makes you as strong as me.

You my dear girl, have been the one who saved me, saved me from endless fears any human being could have, fears that believe me you only hear about that end up in tragedy. You will never know how much you did to save your dad, but I am going to explain all in this story. I am just so thankful I had you by my side, I am so thankful you are such a daddy's girl, you are the sole reason I've managed to somehow get through this struggle, and stayed out of trouble.

I just want you to picture the moment I began to write this story, because I want to set you in the mood that maybe I was in, just so you may have a feeling of how I felt. It's late at night, in a house that is quiet, in a house I hate because all I see and feel within the house are images that show me what a fool I was, images that show me exactly what I've lost more then what I have gained. I have no friends and my family are unaware of the pain I have inside my heart and the questions I have keep spinning in my head and never stop as I have no answers to anything I want to know.

You're laying by my side, your fast asleep unaware of what's happening to your family, unaware of how your dad, a man who is your comfort blanket, is truly feeling. I felt like a bad dad, like I let you down when I couldn't find faults in anything I ever did.

I NEVER DID ANYTHING WRONG

I feel lonely and in need to speak to someone, but I have no one I can turn to, in my eyes I have no one who is willing to listen or even help without them continuously rubbing my one mistake in my eyes. This is a mistake I did for my family, a mistake because I wanted the best for you. That mistake was leaving all my friends and family, putting more stress my way all for the sake of what your mum wanted, in other words I trusted your mum, trusted that she wanted the best for you too. Most of the people I know if I spoke to them will continuously tell me that they were right and that I should have listened to them, how can I ever confide in people like this? These are the people that have made me shut away from the world.

It's at this moment feeling lonely and anxious to talk when I reached for my laptop to write a story to express my feelings, but I didn't know how to start, and I still didn't know why I wanted to write down what happened. Surly me writing down my thoughts would make me feel worse so I put the laptop down and gave you a kiss and cuddled next to you to sleep. About five minutes later it dawned on me, you were the reason for me to write, I had a reason to write my story, a story that would show you who your dad was, a story to make you feel proud of your dad, as he did everything and anything for you.

I originally began to write the story in chapters, and like a fictional story, however I didn't like the way it was coming out. It made no sense to me as I read it back, it had no structure, it seemed made up, I couldn't feel my emotion in my writing, in fact the type of writing I was doing was incredibly hard for me to do, I had to think what I was writing, I just wanted my writing to just flow out my mind.

What made it worse was that as I wrote, more and more things were being aimed at me, more circumstances were being created that were making me fade away, some which ultimately made me give up on the book because emotionally I was drained, emotionally some would say I gave up on everything.

THIS STORY IS REAL NOT FICTIONAL

The thought that maybe one day I will die and leave your side sunk in to my thoughts, I couldn't leave your side and for you to be none the wiser of what had happened. I somehow regained the energy within myself to begin my story so I could tell you again. I thought long and hard how to write my story, my story was real, in no way was it fictional and in no way could I write my story in chapters, my story couldn't be broken down, this story was and will always be one continuous interlinking story.

I then realised the book was for you, I stopped thinking about anyone else that may read the book, and I thought about how I would tell you, which brings me to the way I have chose to and have written this story. It's me, your daddy telling you my daughter his story.

I've left the story real, which means the occasional grammar and maybe the occasional word used is not politically correct, but you know what? I really don't care, this story as I said is about me telling you, and it's all my emotion coming from my heart, it's my inner thoughts. The words and the way I tell you are about how and who I am, and not how the world perceives how it should and must be written, if that's what they want, then they should go and get a best seller. So please bear in mind as you read on, the story you will read has parts written as it was happening to me, there may be circumstances you will read and think that my thoughts are very harsh, a bit extreme, but at that particular time that is exactly how I felt and I am never going to hide away from how low I was, to be honest, I've read everything back to myself on numerous occasions and everything I've written is still something I believe in, it's to show you how far I was pushed. Remember everything I do and will do is for you, you are my life, I will not say sorry for saying something I believe in or doing something I would fight for.

It's my heart telling you this story

No matter what happens or has happened, I've been the best dad I possibly can, I have always been there for you, and I have always put you first. Never ever hate me for telling you this story as I feel that would be the biggest blow in my life, maybe a blow that could and would take me over the edge one day.

You really are the best thing in my life, although I moan about my life, and the lifestyle I have been given to live, ultimately I've also been blessed with the best possible thing in the world, and of course that can only be you. As for the crap in my life, I need to be positive and I am aware that no storm lasts forever; the sun must come up one day, and it must dry these tears.

Obviously I gave my story to a selected few people that I could trust to read in various stages within my writing, this was in aid to help me correct my story in regards to little mistakes that I may have not seen.

Little did they know I was also after some feedback on how they felt about the book, I wanted to see if they felt the emotion I had within this book, I wanted to see how they would react to the truth, the truth that none were aware of. I thank the few people I selected to read the story, and I thank them for the feedback given, even though they were unaware they were giving me it, I really do appreciate your time, it means so much to me.

I've included some of the comments from these people, I've included these comments to show you and to give you an insight to what you are about to read. One word of advice I can give is that maybe you should have a box of tissues nearby; everyone has told me they were in tears at stages within the book, and as this book is for you, I'm sure you will shed some tears, because to you this story is as real as it gets, it's your life in writing, it's your dad who went to war for you.

HERE'S THE FEEDBACK

"I can't finish the book, I'm sorry. It's to hurtful to know
you went through this, I can't read any more"

"You didn't just write a story. You laid your heart bare. Do you know
how courageous that is? It's about time that the parents who have
been screwed over speak out and show that you are human too"

"All I can say is that if my dad did this, I'll be so proud of him,
and I know how important it is for you that your daughter is proud
of you, you really are the best dad in the world. Well done"

"Your daughter is very lucky to have you"

"It's sad and upsetting and makes me mad and angry at the same time"

"This is the start of something special.
This story will touch many people's hearts"

"It's very hurtful to know you've been treated like that and I only need
to read it to understand how hard you fought for things to work out"

"I'm telling you, no one will protect you more
than that little girl as she gets bigger"

I hope you're ready to read, in saying that I doubt there will ever be a time where you are ready, but there has to be a moment in time in your life where you will have to. No matter what, you will never be alone, daddy will always be watching, forever protecting and my love will never die, and I will always be there for you whenever and wherever we may be. As you read this never feel alone, I am here for you always, as silly as a question may feel, or as emotional as you may feel whether its good or bad, happy or sad, come to me as I will be there for you always. I will never turn my back on you, I never have and I never intend to, just remember that wherever you may be in your life, or however you may feel, daddy will always help.

I KNOW THERE WILL NEVER BE A TIME WHERE YOU WILL BE READY TO READ THIS

You may ask why I have called this book EXPOSED? Well in my eyes and in my heart I feel I've gone from being strong, too weak. I've managed through my own choice through trust of people to put my guard down which allowed me to become exposed to things and circumstances that I never wanted; these in turn brought me to my lowest. But it also means that I am now exposing everything, so the word exposed in this particular sense has two meanings, what happened to me and what I am about to do. Now I could immediately point fingers right now at the start of this story aiming them at particular people, but it wouldn't make sense to you, you need to hear the whole story as it developed. I understand if I blame someone now, without you knowing the whole story, you will begin to judge those people and I don't want you doing that, I want you to digest the story, feel my thoughts and feelings and understand what I was going through, trying and doing everything I possibly could to stop the world falling apart in front of me. I also want to say this, I know there are many people worse off than me, so please don't think that I'm singling myself to be the unluckiest guy in the world, I know I am not. I just want my story told to maybe one day make sense to you, and maybe help others who may find themselves in my position, maybe I have a voice, and maybe this is why I have lived my life the way I have. So let me start this story, and I'll start it all in true fairy tale fashion.

ONCE UPON A TIME

Once upon a time, I had everything, I was happy, people didn't play games with me, and most importantly I didn't have to think too deeply about what was around the corner and what was coming my way. I had no responsibilities away from work, everyone in my life was someone that I trusted and more importantly they trusted me. To me that is what I call respect; unfortunately not many people show that trait anymore.

In the eyes of some, I was the man everyone envied, the guy everyone wanted to follow, but to be honest the ones who wanted to follow me where the ones who didn't know the real me, they only knew me from a distance. I found someone in your mum who I thought I could trust, I allowed her into my world, and allowed her to share who I was. Little did I know that some people just play games because they have a bigger picture down the end of their journey, and in fact they will do anything and everything possible to get what they want, not caring about anything or anyone beyond themselves. They play the trust card, and as soon as they get to the stage where they know that person is vulnerable and helpless, they will go for the kill, and show no emotion, guilt, pride or respect towards anyone but themselves.

This is what I mean by exposed, the moment you let your guard down, that's the moment you are exposed to losing who you are, what you are and what you're going to be. You are probably the only person in this world where I have never changed who I am for, I have and will always be me around you the person I am, the person I want to be, I have no reason to be fake with you. To others, who can be friends, family, work colleagues or customers I tend to think or act differently around them, all because either they don't understand me, they can't understand me, they won't understand me or for the simple reason I just can't be bothered with them.

NO ONE CAN OR WILL UNDERSTAND

I've lived a horrible 2013 where I saw everything I lived for crumble away from me, and without you around I wouldn't have wanted to live it. I also know a very hard 2014 is on its way and only God knows what the years to follow will be like. But as for now the time has come for me to expose why I've been exposed, believe me someone is bound to get exposed, and I'm beginning the process by telling my precious little girl everything.

I know some people will think I'm being out of order with what I am about to write, some will think you have no right to know any of the facts I am about to share. If they don't like it, then they can stop reading now, as I said this story is for you. In my eyes, I am your father, I have never hurt you or ever let you down, and I never intend to. I want to teach you to always tell the truth and if I can't tell you the truth of what's happened to us, then I won't be preaching what I believe in, or as some say, lead by example. Something I want you to do with me is to never lie to me, as lies will only hurt the ones who love you most, and in return I promise I will never lie to you, and I will always tell you the truth, if you upset me, I will tell it straight to your face, because to me that's what life is all about, being there for the people who mean the most to you and always being true to them. I am sure there will be times as you grow up you will hate me because I'll say something or disagree with some of your actions that you have done, but I know that's part of being the best dad I can for you.

Look at it this way, if what I am about to write is going to sound out of order, then the people that did it, the people who acted irresponsibly towards both of us shouldn't have done it, and there would have been no need to write this story. In fact I truly wish I was writing you a book titled "Daddy's Lucky Princess" but unfortunately this is no happy story. It's kind of ironic I say this, as I did begin to write a collection of children's book which were titled with your name and the adventure you had within the story, but your mums actions made me stop after five stories, and the stories never ever left the page I wrote them on, maybe one day I will be able to finish the collection. However for this story I will make it my responsibility to make it a happy ending, not for my sake, but for yours.

EXPLAIN HOW ONE EYE CAN CREATE A RIVER TO FLOOD THE WORLD?

This book is dedicated to you, my daughter, for identity reasons I will not name you, or any other person within this story, although I am aware that if this book and story does get told to the world, I'm somehow convinced that they will somehow find a way and put names and faces to the people I speak about. For me as I write this, the only goal, the only focus I have is my story to you, to describe exactly what we went through together, for you to understand exactly who your dad is, and why I am who I am. To me the names are not important; this story is about me and you and no one else.

I will admit that I do have an ambition and a goal to try and publish this story, I do have my reasons for this mainly because a few people who knew I was doing this told me that I should, they told me that it's a story that many people would identify themselves within and also because I feel that this story needs to be told and needs people out in the world who are clueless to people's lives who seem normal but struggling to actually have an insight and a little understanding that people are getting used and hurt for no good reasons. I use to be blind to what I've been through, now it's happened to me I am very confident that there are far too many parents in my situation, and it's about time someone stood up to these bully's. Yes, I agree the word bully is a very strong word to use, but believe me there is no other word that I can think of or find that can best describe what has been aimed my way by certain people.

IT'S THE ONLY WORD I CAN THINK OF THAT I CAN USE

These parents have had to keep quiet and possibly lose everything, which could be their own child, the upsetting thing for me is that their own child would never know the truth, and sometimes the justice system in place would never have the appropriate outcome for the child in question, so this is why certain parents in my eyes just keep quiet. Believe me when I say this, I will fight for you and fight for what I own till my last breath makes it impossible for me to do otherwise.

Maybe I can and should start a campaign from completion of this book, to try and get wrong doing parents put in their place and the people who actually do the right things rewarded in some way. I have no idea how this could be done, but this is me thinking out loud.

As this story, in my eyes, is a story that no child regardless of who they are is a story they should never hear. It's worse for me because I have written it and it's for my own child. My daughter should never ever have had to hear this story or be part of it. So with this thinking, if and this is a big if, if I can get someone to publish and represent me, I pledge that I will never ever accept any royalties for this book, if I do manage to get this published, then I pledge that all profits made from this book will be shared between you and children's based charities, one being the Make-A-Wish Foundation and the other being the NSPCC.

One thing I have learnt since your birth is that all children are innocent, all children deserve more in this world then what the world can give them. The world we live in is so corrupt in many ways and forms and unfortunately this corruption if we as adults, parents, and ultimately as human beings don't act correctly will one day lead the whole race as humans to a degree that we don't care about anything but ourselves, and as sad as this sounds not even care about our own blood that we have created.

SO MANY THINGS IN THIS WORLD ARE CORRUPTED

Children deserve to be brought up in happy surroundings, with no stress, no knowledge or thought about anything but learning and having fun. I, hand on heart believe that all children deserve to be a child and live their only care free period of their life care free. This is why I choose the Make-A-Wish Foundation as a chosen charity as they help sick children share memories of making their wishes and dreams with their families come true, something that touches my heart and makes me emotional, love is extremely underestimated in this world, and I mean true love.

The other charity that I want to get some of the profits will be the NSPCC; this is a charity whose mission is to end cruelty to children. Brining you up the way I have, I have learnt how delicate you are to your surroundings, how you mimic and learn what and who is around you, in particular to new and interesting things you may have not experienced before. I also am fully aware of how the environment you are brought up in can and will impact your future. Every child needs the opportunity to live a normal happy life in a caring environment, and in a place where they are never under threat verbally and physically. I understand every charity in this world is worthy, but to me these two charities relate to my life as I speak, these two charities are what I am trying to do for you, trying to give you a happy care free life, and trying to make all your dreams and wishes come true every day.

Some may say, and even you may say, although I may personally not pursue any percentage of the profits, why have I included you in my wish list to receive some? Well here is the answer, I know I am not going to be around forever, my story I hope will. Your mum in particular, as you read, will discover has ruined your future plans, because I don't know what tomorrow will hold for you. I want to make sure I've left you something behind. Now as you get older it's up to you if you feel that you wish to share your money with worthy charities, but that will be your decision and whatever you decide to do, I will support you all the way.

If I am unable to get someone to represent me, because I know I am an unknown, because I know my story is very raw or because people may not understand it. If this is the case then I will self publish my book, I will spend my own money to try and get my story out into the world, if I do manage to do this, then I obviously will take royalties to pay for all the costs I have had to pay out, after I have recouped all these funds, I again will pledge my royalties to my chosen charities.

My story is going to explain to you the things I have had to deal with just so you know that daddy's always been there in the past and that I will forever be there in the future. The importance of the story is the love and care that is shown from both of us, as well as the story of your proud dad; it's a never ending bond that will last forever.

I CAN'T CHANGE THE PAST

Yes, there's going to be many circumstances where I explain what other people do, in particular your mum, and I need to add this bit in here before you read any further into the story. I never intended to use this as a medium to bring down your mum; I used this as a medium to firstly help me not go insane by expressing my internal thoughts. Secondly I want to leave you answers for questions you may have, but most importantly I want you to have a dad who will be around for you in the flesh as you grow and learn because if I didn't speak out, I have no idea what would have happened. I also want you to be proud of me and hopefully one day fully understand that your dad will never ever let you down. I am someone you can trust with anything and everything in this hurtful world. I after completion of writing this story, read the story back to myself over and over again, it may seem all I did was bad mouth and moan about your mum. But, it's what's happened, I can't change what happened because that's now the past, and I for one can't hide from the truth.

I never want this story to make you hate your mum, or even make the world hate her, but unfortunately there is no way to make your mum sound good, and everything I explain in this story has it's reasons and it's explanations. I've wrote you my story, what I went through, but I needed to show and describe to you how my life was, and how difficult and what a struggle physically and mentally it has been. But unfortunately it was mostly to do with your mum's actions and thinking's; they were the main cause to my spiral downfall.

Your mum has never made me being a dad to you easy, in fact she has made the pleasurable task of being a dad near impossible, maybe to the brink of sometimes me asking myself if it was worth it. I feel I have succeeded, and believe I've dealt with everything that was thrown my way in a professional manner that never harmed or impacted you. Another thing you need to realise is that everything I have written is something that I myself have either seen, heard, thought or most importantly felt.

15

Your mum must have thought I had no feelings to which is why she continued doing what she had done, either that or she was so dumb she thought she would never get caught.

I NEVER WANT YOU TO HATE YOUR MUM

Most dads in my position would have walked away, and believe me I would normally be the first to bring down the fathers that left their children so they could start a new life, but when reality hits you, when crap continuously happens to you and you can never see an ending to it all, it's only then you begin to have an insight to what these people may have gone through. When things happen to you, no one outside the four walls of your life, and in most cases no one outside the cavity of your own skull will believe your story, as well as no one supporting you, and to top it all off, all you get is stress and strain, sometimes you have no option but just to walk away. This story is to show you why I should have walked, but more importantly why I haven't and never will. You need to realise everything I say in this book is me explaining to you what I've had to deal with, so you can realise how much I have had to deal with and what I had to go through on my own, but it won't end here. I know I will forever go through what I am going through, this book is designed to take you inside my mind, to see my deepest internal thoughts, thoughts and feelings that people didn't know I had. Just because someone smiles, and tries to joke and laugh every day at every occasion, that does not mean they have no feelings, that doesn't mean that they are happy and have no worries. From my experience people who act like this, are usually someone trying to hide away from the truth, for some strange reason, fake smiles fool many people. I am going to tell you things I did that I didn't even tell my own family because I felt I was in all this mess alone and had no idea on how to ask for help.

No matter what I write and what you read and hear, they will never describe how much love and care I have for you, although I have gone through stages where I was unable to see you every day and I know that in the future there will be more of these dreadful days coming, you need to realise it was never my intention, this was never my fault to be away from you, because if it was up to me, I'd be by your side every second of the day, and it kills me when I'm away from you. In my eyes you have been taken away from the one person you feel safe with, the one person you trusted from the moment you were born, I know deep down what has happened and will happen will affect you as you get older, but no one is prepared to listen to a dad in my position and I mean no one, not even the authorities.

This is my story to show you what I went through, what I had to and still have to deal with. My life will never ever be the same and no matter how hard I try I will never be the same person I use to be.

The introduction of you into my life should have been the start of a beautiful life that I could only dream about, but as I write this book, that dream is far, far away and I am convinced as a father and you as my daughter, that dream will never be a reality.

I also want to dedicate this book to every father out there that is wrongly accused and is walked over by the mother of their children, all because mothers think they have more power than the father. Fathers are just as important then mothers, and the whole world needs to realise and register this in their own head. I'm here to prove some mothers have their own game play and it's not their child's best interest, whether they know it or not, or whether they just act dumb is regardless of the situation at hand. I also dedicate this to all good mothers out there, I know there are a few, maybe many, they are the reason why I still believe that maybe one day I'll find a caring female which will be nice to me and someone that will respect I have a beautiful daughter and be nice to you. As for all the parents both mums and dads who don't deserve to have children, how do you look at yourselves in the mirror every day? People like you disgust me, and as I said I would love to start a campaign to start bringing you all down one by one, you never know, maybe just maybe I will get that opportunity one day.

I WILL NEVER GET BACK TOGETHER WITH YOUR MUM

I have had to write this story because I have no one I can go to, I have no one that will listen but more importantly understand why I do the things I do, I am at a stage of my life where thoughts and fears run through my head and make me feel sick. I can't ask for help from people, as I don't want to seem weak, but my side of the story now needs to be heard, I also desperately want to write this for you, because deep down I know you'll hate me for saying I will never ever get back together with your mum even if your mum pleads on her knees for forgiveness, it will never happen. It hurts me to say you will never have that family life I wanted you to have, but I've wrote this so you can understand why you can't, but you need to understand you will always be my main priority no matter where I may be or what I may be doing.

When and if I find someone else to be with, they must accept I have a daughter, but both you and her will have to understand I have enough love for everyone, and understand it's not a contest to get my attention, the person I am, I will always sacrifice myself for the ones I love, you will always have that, but I hope there will be a time when there will be someone else as well. I hope there is someone out there, I say this because a friend of mine told me that the only way for me to trust this world again and for me to be free, is to find love away from you, to be able to get close to someone again, to understand that someone will be there in my corner rather than being against me all the time. They told me only then will I have true smiles, smiles that will make me happy, and maybe complete, apparently I deserve that, apparently I deserve to forget my past and start thinking of the future ahead that I may have, but at the moment when I think of the future I feel sick, as it's just a blank, because tomorrow is exactly the same as what it is today and is exactly the same as every other day I have lived for a very long time now. But please when the time comes, never get jealous, you will always be daddy's princess, no matter how old you are.

BEING A DAD IS THE BEST THING IN THE WORLD, ESPECIALLY TO YOU

Being a GOOD father is without a doubt the hardest job in the world, but to me it is not a job, it is a pleasure. So to me being a father is the most satisfying thing in the world. Please note I did state GOOD in capitals when I said being a father was the hardest job, and I guess that works for both set of parents, being a GOOD mother should also be the hardest job or pleasure depending on how you look at it. However some parents don't appreciate what they have, they believe being called a mum or even a dad is enough and use this status as a way of getting what they want, when they want it. In my case it's more so with the mum, because of the power that mum's seem to have over the dad's within this crazy law that we have to obey and live within. I throughout my time of trying to do what was right for you were constantly told by your mum that she had more rights because she was a mum and that I couldn't do anything about it, because if I did, she would take you away from me. How do you think that makes me feel? I always had to obey every wish and demand your mum made, even though it was putting me and you out. But I did it as a father, because you needed me to be there for you, and that's what I did.

No one knows what tomorrow holds, but hopefully my side of the story can and will be shared and told.

To all those people who may read this, to all those who said I was being silly, to those who told me your mum was not worth stressing about, you will all now hear the truth; you will now see what I went through, and what I had to deal with on my own, and only now you will all realise just how strong I actually was. I never ever stressed for your mum once, I actually got over the fact we were over fairly quickly, but instead stressed for being made to look like a fool over and over again, as well as your mum using you against me over and over again and by her doing this I felt extremely uncomfortable of how you was and would be brought up. Believe me I'm no angel, I don't want you to ever think I am, I know that no one in this world is perfect, everyone has their own flaws, but one thing I am, and one thing that I am proud of is that I am true to who I am, and true to the ones I love and true to the ones who are there for me.

Your mum thought I'd never tell the truth, your mum thinks I'm stupid and I don't know the games she plays, well guess what? It's all coming out now. Although I hate people judging others, after reading this I don't want people to hate your mum, but she deserves to be judged and I hope everyone, including strangers all across the world talk about her behind her back, because that's exactly what happened to me. I want people to judge this unknown mum they read about in this story, I want everyone to talk about her, and for her to look small without anyone knowing who she really is. When people judged me they just looked at me, they felt sorry for me, but they never helped or spoke to me, all they did was gossip behind my back, believing what they heard. That's what your mum's actions did to me; I hated it, I didn't confront these people because it's not my style, they can believe what they want, they can think of me as they wish, I just didn't want to bring anymore stress into my corner by approaching and arguing with these people, instead I knew I was bigger and better then what they thought I was. I just happily smiled and got on with my day pretending nothing was happening and nothing was hurting me inside.

JUST BECAUSE SOMEONE SMILES, IT DON'T MEAN THEY ARE HAPPY

I know it's really bad of me saying this, but you'll soon realise on reading this story why I'm saying this, I was judged when I did nothing wrong, your mum surly deserves to be judged, especially with everything wrong that she has done. As for you, promise me you'll never hate your mum, remember it's your dad's wish that you don't, and you don't want to upset me now do you?

Whoever reads this, and in particular yourself, I don't want anyone to ever feel sorry for me, maybe have some sympathy for me but never any sorrow. Every decision I have made has brought me to where I am today, it brought me to you or you to me, that alone my dear girl is by far the greatest decision I ever made. I had options to everything I did, but I chose to do the right thing at that time, the right thing may not have been for me, it was never for anybody but you, so bear in mind when reading this, understand you were my only factor in any decision making I did. I don't want people to ever feel sorry for me for what the outcome was, because I know when I look at you, and I get that hug, every decision, every heartbreak, every bit of stress, tiredness and pain I got, was worth it.

TIME FOR THE EXPOSED TO EXPOSE!

A big reason to why I've wrote this is because I know that one day as you get older you will without a doubt begin to start to ask questions. These are questions that maybe no one will ever give you the truth to, questions that maybe will make no sense in your mind, and answers to which will confuse you even more then you may feel. I know one day you'll have the question, why is mum not with dad? Well this is my side of the story. What I as a father worry about most is that maybe I won't be around to give you the answers from my side, which is why I'm now writing my thoughts. I'm also terrified I won't be around for you to hear the truth and also for the fact that I won't be around to see you grow and learn makes the pain I suffer twice as bad. Deep down within me I am also scared my love will never be justified or realised by you and never realised fully by me the love you have for me. I know you love me; you show it to me every day, maybe innocent love from a child is actually somewhat better then actually hearing from an adult that they love you, because as an adult you learn the trait of lies.

If, God forbid, something does happen to me and I disappear and I was unable to ever say goodbye or unable to give you a goodbye kiss, please accept that it must have been out of my hands, I will never leave you of my own will. As you will read, I went through torture to make sure you were fine and my love for you will never ever die, in fact the love I have somehow gets stronger daily, which is impossible to believe considering how much I love you already. I know the pain I've gone through since your second birthday will never be topped, only unless you become ill and I can't do nothing to protect you, but god forbid that will ever happen, I would rather die than ever let anything happen to you.

The moment I found out your mum was pregnant was the day I stopped and became serious about the people I wanted in my life. I had a real focus on where I was going. Yes your mum fell pregnant early on in our relationship, and yes I understand your mum was young. In fact you were the second time your mum fell pregnant, the first was unfortunately aborted because your mum felt she was too young, and as much as I wanted to keep the baby, I allowed your mum to do what she wished for. The more I think about it now; I really do wonder if that baby was even mine. Regardless of that thought, that really should have been a sign to me to tell me to be more careful, but I wasn't, and I'm glad I wasn't, because your mum fell pregnant with you. And no matter how much stress and agony I have been through, you are the shining star that makes all this stress and grief I go through worthwhile.

Your mum had to move into my house, luckily I owned a house all by myself, it wasn't a problem, I did everything I could to make sure your mum was happy and comfortable. If she wanted this, and she wanted that, at whatever time it was, I did it. Your mum no matter how stubborn she is, she herself cannot deny I didn't do any of her wishes. The only thing that I will accept is that I spent far too much time at work; this wasn't through choice but due to my position as a store manager in a high street supermarket. I had responsibilities, I had duties, I couldn't just get up and go and ignore the things that gave me money to pay for everything she wanted, but also the money that allowed me to give you the best possible upbringing.

I'm hoping this story will be a realisation to show you who I was, how I was, what I was, but most importantly a story to show you, I never wanted to let you down, I never wanted you to be unhappy. All I ever wanted and still want is for you to be the happiest girl in the world.

ALL I WANT IS FOR YOU TO BE HAPPY

Being free is something I sacrificed not just for you, but also for your mum. When I say free, I mean doing things that I want to do, I hardly see my family, your hala, your uncle, your nene, your cousins as well as my close cousins. Family is a massive thing for me, but I was putting everything I had into my own made family, but at the same time I was hurting my own family and myself because I was beginning to become distant from them. It's no wonder then I felt awkward when they came to my aid when I was at my lowest, I felt embarrassed I choose an outsider, a fake over my own flesh and blood. I would only see my family on special occasions, for me to not see my brother was a big thing for me, I used to see him three to four times a week, even if it was just for half an hour, it allowed me to see him and speak to him. I also became distant from your cousins, these three kids that mean a lot to me, I wasn't in their lives any more, I wasn't seeing them grow up.

But why? Why wasn't I seeing them?

YOU NEED TO HAVE YOUR OWN THOUGHTS

Whatever I write will always be taken out of context, and there is nothing I can say or do that will prevent this, but what I will say is, although what I write may seem as if I make your mum to be the worst person in the world, you need to have your own thoughts. In my eyes your mum is my enemy, the one person I hate more than anything, but she is your mum and that should never ever be lost in translation. I'm also a firm believer that it is important to have both parents by your side no matter what happens. However your mum has her own thoughts and more than likely will have her own stories to tell, and no matter what I say, and what you read, it's just my side of the story. But I want to show you, I did nothing wrong, my priority was you, then your mum; my needs never came into question or consideration. But I do warn you now, I know your mum well, I know all her traits, she will deny everything, she will get moody if you ask questions, she will go cold when caught out doing something wrong, so please don't ever expect answers from your mum, you'll never get the truth. In fact if your mum ever reads this book, she will deny everything, tell you she was the best mum in the world, tell you I was crazy, tell you I was insane, and that everything being told was being made up in my head. But that's what your mum does, she plays a very political card, when instead I choose the option of being there for you when you need it most and most importantly when you don't need any help at all, maybe this is why you always run to me rather than your mum when you hurt yourself or even when you just want to play.

I GAVE UP EVERYTHING BECAUSE OF YOUR MUM

So why wasn't I spending time with my family? The fact is, your mum was demanding, wanting this and that to be done, and with very little time away from work, this could only be done in my spare time, spare time which may I add was very rare at the best of times, this is time in which I would have liked to spend with my family, friends or even my close cousins. I even stopped playing football every Sunday morning because your mum's needs were too great and I just didn't have the time. Most people will argue that you can make time if you want, but hand on heart the longer the time I knew your mum the less time I had. Which brings me to the position I am in now, spare time is something I hear about and know of, I have no idea what that is now. If I was asked to go out with my mates, she would always make me feel low and horrible. If I asked us to go out as a family she would not want to do it unless she suggested it, your mum has always been content sitting on her backside and doing nothing, anything that may be effort is not worth her time. One instance pops into my mind as I try to explain this, it was a Sunday afternoon when Arsenal were due to take on Tottenham, I really wanted to watch this football match, obviously due to the rivalry of the two sides, as well as me and your uncle both being Arsenal fans. I asked to go and watch it at your uncle's house; I asked if she could have you for a few hours whilst I went to watch it, she was adamant she would come as well; I had nothing against it so we all went. It really got to me, your mum has no interest in football and you were running around causing a mess in someone else's house. It was not just because of the mess, it was more to do with your own safety, I asked her a few times to look after you, she didn't budge. Your mum just sat on the sofa as she looked through her phone and made me run around after you. This is what it was like all the time, everything is an effort for her unless there is something worthwhile at the end. Surly her own daughter should have been reason enough? As well as allowing me to actually have some down time with my brother and allowing us to watch the match and have a catch up in peace.

NOTHING IN THE WORLD CAN GIVE YOU MORE JOY, THEN THE SMILE ON YOUR CHILD'S FACE

The day you were born, I was so happy, I was the first guy in the world to ever see you, first guy in the world to ever hold you and kiss you, The moment you was born, the extreme worrying began, I was scared, were you ok? But as soon as I heard your cry, I knew you were fine, you were beautiful, and I knew at that moment when I was holding you; there could never be anything in the world that would ever be more precious to me then you. I knew the stress and pain that was going to come was going to be intense, for crying out loud I worry about my niece and nephews all the time, especially when they get ill, you were going to give me a hundred times, if not more, stress than they ever have.

So you came home that very day, both your mum and me were so nervous, we had no idea what to do, we were both new to this. I know I hardly slept a wink that evening, I was too excited but very worried that something may happen, you may need something and I wasn't there to help you.

I was so happy, I was tired but happy, I had a family, your mum, you and me, that's all I wanted, that's all I needed, it made me complete, and it's strange for me to say that. The truth is I never wanted kids, I never really wanted to ever find anyone I could have a family with, but having what I had in front of me just opened my eyes, made me see that this is what life was all about. Your mum in the first nine months of your birth was perfect. Whilst on her maternity leave she looked after you well, she put my needs in to place and allowed me to rest when needed, everyone I knew was so proud of your mum, saying how good she was. Don't get me wrong, she made a few mistakes, but we were first time parents, these were expected. Even your nene, the hardest person to please was amazed at how good and well your mum looked after you. Even when your mum went back to work after her maternity ended, she would come back home at lunch to make sure you was ok.

I CAN'T AND WON'T FORGET ANYTHING

Although I thought your mum was amazing at first, the mistakes she was making began to leave scars in my thoughts, as they were too frequent and these are mistakes that really shouldn't have been happening if she was fully concentrating on you. These are scars that in time would make me worry so much that I couldn't and wouldn't ever be able to fully relax when I was away from you, knowing that you were with your mum. Little things like your mum locking you in her car with the keys still in the car whilst she went to the zoo with her friend; she had to phone the fire brigade to smash the window open. Even things like your mum leaving super glue on the floor, allowing you to crawl to it to stick your hands together, but it weren't just your hands, you put the glue in your mouth and god knows how much of it you ate. You're mums careless attitude was shown when she used adult bonjela rather than the children's version even though I made it clear where the child's version was kept, or what about bathing you with a sponge that was used with bleach to clean the bath, these are all little things that always play on my mind. I was always told by your mum when they happened not to worry, but it was always me that took it seriously, it was always me that phoned the NHS hotline and asked for advice, even when you was sick, but as time went on, as you got older, these situations just got worse, to the extent that when I had to work and you were with your mum I would worry, now when you was with nene or even with nanny I wouldn't, because I've seen how they are with you and I am comfortable of how they look after you, I am confident that they will watch every step you make, and am sure they won't let anything happen to you. Unfortunately worrying is something that will never go away from me when it comes to you, not even when you get older, be warned, and I warn you now, every guy will be questioned when they come near you in the future.

Things between your mum and me were never perfect all the time. But isn't that life? Not everything is good all the time, but I knew in time our relationship would get better, I was adamant that time was what we needed. We both worked full time, we had you to look after in the evenings. (Before you say anything, you was never ever at fault for our breakdown) Your nene would look after you whilst we worked, but the thing that got me was that your mum got to a stage of her life where she wouldn't look after you, wouldn't cook, would clean once in a while and that's only if someone was coming round so she could make an impression, otherwise she would just sit and watch her reality TV programmes. I deep down hated these because I could see your mum wanting what she saw on TV, these programmes were all scripted and not real. I didn't understand how anyone could want what was being shown, all your mum watched and saw were single girls partying all the time, sleeping with anyone they liked, no worries, no stress, but the thing that wound me up even more, although most people in the world knew these programmes were fake, she would think they were real. At nights when you would wake up, ninety-nine times out of hundred it would be me that would come to your attention, and at times this would be three to four times a night. I ended up sleeping on the hard floor next to your crib because I was just so tired from my long minimum twelve hour nonstop shift at work, as well as looking after you and your mum.

I NEVER HAD A DECENT NIGHT SLEEP

But being the dad I was, being the guy I was to your mum I was ok with it, I wanted your mum to be happy, and I was more than happy to look after you. With all this in mind, your mum wanted to move houses, I didn't have an issue with this as I always wanted you to live and allow you to grow up outside of London, but the issue I had was, the move would put more stress on me, I was moving away from my mum, the woman who looked after you when both me and your mum went work, it was going to be my responsibility to drop you off and pick you up every day. But it was also going to put strain on my journey to work and home, this was now adding on average, an extra ninety minutes a day to my journey.

Even before we moved houses I was struggling, I had to see the doctors because I was so tired, The doctors had to send me to get a blood test, but even then your mum still turned a blind eye to my needs, I asked for help, I told her I was tired, the response I got from her not once but on two occasions are responses that echo in my ear over and over again. As well as hearing your mum's response, she also mimicked her response at me, again an image that I can't delete out my head, an image that makes me sick, an image that proves who your mum really is. When I asked for help because I was tired, she told me that she would get her violin out, and that everyone should feel sorry for me because I was tired. After the second time of asking and hearing the same response, I refused to ask for help from her ever again. Your mum was too selfish to help me and was in her own world, I thought looking after your own child, watching them grow up was part of parenthood, but not helping the father out because he may have been tired from doing everything is not a valid reason, is it me or am I right in thinking her thinking is not right? She must have known what she was doing was wrong because she promised she would change if I moved closer to her family, she promised she would spend more time with you and look after you more, she promised her family would help out more, she would help look after the home, in the position I was in, even a little help would have been nice, but on second thoughts knowing everything that I do now, maybe everything she had promised was all a plan to get what she wanted. Maybe it was all a cunning plan that she developed to get what she ultimately wanted. If anything getting a new house made her worse, your mum began to develop an ego problem, like she was the best thing in the world, and everything had to be done for her more than ever before.

YOU'RE MUMS VIOLIN LESSONS AS A CHILD PAID OFF

There were times I asked for her to get up at night if you cried, just to allow me to sleep for a change without interruption, I knew from her body language she didn't want to, but she also said she never ever heard you cry in the nights. I was amazed at how she couldn't, there were times I laid in bed whilst you cried and looked across at your mum, but she just laid there, she didn't flinch, but I knew she was awake, because when I called out her name to wake her up, she just ignored me to pretend she was fast asleep, believe me, your mum heard me, and she heard you, but she was just being her selfish self again. I knew she was pretending to sleep; there is no way she could not hear you cry as well as not hearing me call out for her. So as always it was me that got up; there was no other choice, I was not going to allow you to cry, but I also know you knew this, I know you know it's me that always comes to your aid when you cry.

As you got older and began to speak, it's always daddy you cried out for, a sign to me that proved that you realised who was coming to your aid at all times. This is why I feel I have this special bond with you today, because you know, I'm always there for you; you know I won't let you down.

Your mum now became complacent in the new house not that she ever was anything else. I used to come home tired from work, and I had to cook, all I did was ask your mum to look after you whilst I cooked not just for me, but your mum as well who had been home for the past two hours and done nothing but just sit down and watch TV or go on the internet. You being you would always follow me and come to the kitchen to play with me, yes it was nice, but your mum would just sit on the sofa watching TV or on her phone, I asked her over and over again just to have you for half hour, why couldn't your mum sit down and play with you whilst I cook? Seriously, there is nothing in this world that is better than playing with your own child, getting to know them and seeing them learn, so I just couldn't and still can't understand why she didn't want to do this.

Is her own ego that big that even her own child can't break it? There was even a time, I came in to the lounge from the kitchen to see your mum watching TV, and you nowhere in sight after asking her to keep an eye on you, I found you in the electric cupboard playing with the fuse box, even situations where I go toilet, ask your mum to look after you, only for you to come up the stairs alone with your mum none the wiser, when I questioned her, her simple response was that you had to learn to climb the stairs somehow. My response that should have been said was that maybe your mum should learn to be a mum, but this response never left my mind, never did I dare speak out, or an argument would have started with me being an idiot to thinking your mum was a bad mum, so I left it at that.

HOW BIG IS THAT EGO?

This was getting to a stage now where everything was down to me, it got very serious when I found you on one occasion with knives in your hand, now you can try and visualise and try to understand the stress and strain I was going through, and the fact I had to do everything myself. The only time I had anything to do for myself was when you was asleep, but that was either tidying, cleaning, or washing, then straight to bed because I was shattered, and I knew tomorrow was another day exactly the same of what today had been like.

I lived and am currently living as I write this through one circle that doesn't allow me to have any time to do anything I want to do that may help me relax, this book has taken me over a year to produce my first draft, and that's because I only have ten hours spare time a month for me to actually write it, and those hours are accumulated from my day off from work once a week, as I drop you off at nursery.

I went on holiday with your mum, her cousin and her boyfriend, and of course you, I felt as if I was only on that holiday to be a babysitter for you as well as a bank for your mum. Again I wouldn't have it any other way, but sometimes a little consideration would have been nice, why was it always me that would wake up early to give you breakfast? Why was it your mum that would get all the lay in's? Why was it your mum that would always sit in the sun whilst I had to play with you in the shade and look after you? Don't get me wrong, but this is my opinion, I believe she only wants you when it suits her. She only wants to be a mum because she has to, because she dare not be seen as a failure to others, but behind closed doors, and this may hurt your mum, but the father of her child sees her as a failed mother. Either my expectations of what I expect of a mother are too great or what I say is un-true and in fact she is a wonderful mum.

As for me being a father, I love it, I thrive on being there for you, protecting you, seeing you learn, but it's at its best when I see and feel your love for me.

IT' MUST BE A LUXURY TO BE ABLE TO TAKE YOUR BABYSITTER ON HOLIDAY WITH YOU

Our first holiday as a family should have just been you, your mum and me. No one else should have come because the three of us needed time away from everything and everyone, but others came. I believe it's because your mum wanted her freedom on holiday, and she got it. She had her baby's dad being the baby sitter, so she could have the holiday she wanted with her cousin and her boyfriend, why would she want to look after and care for a baby? It's not what holidays are for; she hardly did it when she was at home. I won't lie, I had enough of your mum on that holiday, there's times I just took you and went for walks, because your mum went in to the sea for hours, or wanted to go topless in the sun as she showed off to her cousin and her boyfriend. She wouldn't and couldn't understand that you were scared being in a complete different place, you were restless, you needed to be comforted, and as we went out for meals it was me that had to do this because as your mum said "I'm on holiday"

There was even a stage I went mad, lost it completely in the streets on holiday, I shouted in your mums face, threw my bottle of water on the floor with force, I must admit I literally lost it, why? This is why. I'd been ignored all holiday, you have only been wanted when it suits her, yet one evening we are sitting outside a bar trying to chill, your mum's cousin and boyfriend are inside the bar playing pool. To me this was a nice thing because it was the first time all holiday that yourself, your mum and me were alone. All your mum did was look inside the bar and watch her cousin and boyfriend, now forgive me that I can't remember what the conversation I was trying to have with your mum was, but under the circumstances it doesn't really matter, because I know I asked the same question five times and got no response. She didn't want to sit there with me and you; she wanted to be inside that bar, so I got up and said I'm going back to the hotel to leave her to be with her cousin and her boyfriend. What she replied was stupid, she said I couldn't take you, even though you were very sleepy, and get this, she demanded I gave her money for drinks and for the cab back to our villa. Well let's just say as I write this story I now know why she was more interested in her cousin and her boyfriend that evening, maybe it's to do with the fact that she was having a fling with her own cousin's boyfriend behind everyone's back.

I AM CONFIDENT EVERY STATEMENT I MAKE IS TRUE

I am confident of that statement because during your mum's twenty first birthday party which she had a few weeks after we returned from holiday, I heard your mum's cousin's boyfriend telling this to some guys. To be honest I'm not sure who these guys were, they could have been friends, his cousins or his own brothers, but they were outside the front of the house as I went to try and find your mum because she had disappeared. Your mum's cousin's boyfriend was telling his mates how your mum was an easy lay, and that how he was still at it with your mum, and for them to try it on with your mum as well, and get this, he was telling them she would be extremely easy that night in the condition that she was in. Yes it was her own party, as she was obviously out of her head and drunk as she danced and lifted other guy's tops up to expose their stomachs.

I HEARD IT WITH MY OWN EARS, AND I SAW IT WITH MY OWN EYES

Little does your mum know, her actions were making me feel small, were making me feel embarrassed as I had my own family present at that party as well. My best mate even questioned me to what your mum was doing, his exact words were "where's her respect towards you?"

But your mum has never had respect towards me, not as a person, and not as the best father she could ever have to any child she may have. During that party it was me, and your nene that constantly checked on you as you slept. But maybe respect is something your mum and her family don't have; do they even know what respect is? Your nanny and grandpa should have told your mum to stop her drunken actions, respect to your mums eldest brother, he did tell the guy she was dancing with to ease off your mum, as I say, I see and hear everything, but was it his duty to be doing this?

WHERE IS THE RESPECT?

As for respect from your mum's cousin and her boyfriend, I actually caught them in my bed having sex as I went up to check on you! My mind does boggle that your mum's cousin's boyfriend is one nasty piece of work, with everything I knew, I should have said it there and then at the party, instead, it being your mums party and not wanting to bring any attention my way I left the room, being told not to mention it to your mum.

It's lucky to say I never saw or met your mum's cousin's boyfriend again after that day, I got a feeling that's a good thing because I have no idea how I would have reacted otherwise.

The more I think about it, and now I am writing this story, my mind really does begin to wonder. Maybe your mum and her cousin's boyfriend were having a fling whilst we were on holiday, maybe your mum disappeared during the party to find him as well, I will never know the answers to any of these questions. But thinking the wrong doing of your mum makes everything else make sense, it's like piecing together a jigsaw puzzle. He didn't stay too long after arriving at the party; maybe he came to give his secret girlfriend a kiss or more? It was him on holiday that tried to calm me down whilst I had my tantrum out on the streets on holiday, he told me that girls are not worth the time and effort us guys put in, and not to make a scene and not to think about it too much, maybe he was scared I was getting too close to the truth. It also kind of makes sense that

34

your mum's cousin and boyfriend were also not one hundred percent on holiday either, but what makes more sense is that your mum was more interested in what they were doing then what me and her own daughter were doing. The thing that got me to have my tantrum that night on holiday was what your mum said to me that she wanted you at that time of night, especially when she really neglected you most of the holiday, and wanting money off me too, money is something that makes your mums eyes open and it's something that she will do anything for. Let me just ask you this, would your mum have a baby for money? Maybe you can answer that question at the end of this story, but whilst you consider the answer, maybe you should know of this.

At the time this was happening like most things, I didn't think much of it, but now, as I think about it, maybe it was all part of the bigger picture, the bigger plan your mum had. Whilst we registered your name, she didn't want my surname on the birth certificate, she only wanted hers, why? This is why you have a hyphened surname which incorporates both our surnames because I wanted you to have mine. But that's not all, your mum asked for me to consider not having my name on the birth certificate, apparently many people were doing it and it was not necessary for me to have mine printed on the certificate. Like most things when you're mum suggested things I kept quiet and agreed but I wasn't prepared to do so on this. I was adamant my name was going on it, but it does make you think, she must have done her research, she must have had this plan in place and I was taken for a ride from day one. Lucky for you, I'm a devoted father and I won't leave your side, unluckily for your mum, she chose the wrong guy to have a kid with because I won't back down when it comes to my daughter.

HOW FAR WOULD YOU GO FOR MONEY?

Anyways, as I said I went mad on holiday, one by-passer had to ask your mum if they wanted them to phone the police for her, I never touched your mum, it was all verbal; apparently your mum was scared. Something about your mum I've recently understood, Your mum gets scared when she tries to get attention from others nearby, just hold that thought, because you'll be shocked when you find out some of the dirt I found, but she also gets scared when she knows she is close to getting caught of wrong doing, or maybe she got scared or wanted me to react to disturb her cousin and her boyfriend getting close to each other and get herself back involved in their circle of fun.

I've thought long and hard about telling your mum what I knew, I've even thought about embarrassing her in front of her own family as well as telling her cousin everything I know, but what good would that do? In fact I believe it could start a war, and to me my focus is you and nothing will get in that way. Your mum is all lies anyway, so she would obviously always deny anything and everything. As for your mum's cousin's boyfriend, what would he say? Again I've thought long and hard about this, he wouldn't want any of his dirty laundry put in the public eye, he would either deny he ever said it or say he was only saying it to make himself look big in front of the people he said it too. However my gut feeling and my knowledge is never wrong, I know what my eyes saw, my ears know what they heard and I know in my thoughts that no matter what anyone tries to tell me, your mum and him were at it behind everyone's back.

So what happened between your mum and me, what brought us to the end? It was Christmas 2012, Christmas is always the busiest time of year for me at work, and I need to be at work longer and without days off. Your mum had just got her new phone, she had downloaded these games one of which was called words, it's like a scrabble based game, a game in which I sometimes played with some of my mates. I never had time off at the best of days, and with it being Christmas I literally had no time to play, even when I did play her, she would always get upset because I would constantly beat her, she would always start accusing me of cheating by sourcing words off the internet, and to be honest I just didn't have time for this childish behaviour. It's at this moment when I suggested she play a guy who I worked with at work, he was someone who I got on well with, and to me mentally they were at the same sort of intelligence within that game play as they were both poor at playing it. The relationship I had with this guy was normal, I would tell this guy things about myself and he would tell me things about him, it was just a normal healthy friendship, there was nothing unusual about it, that's what guys do. I knew he was a genuine player mind, but I thought no way would he try anything with his boss's girl and I thought no way would your mum put her family at risk for a no body, especially when you consider we had only been in our new home for just five months.

DON'T EVER THINK YOU WON'T GET CAUGHT, BECAUSE YOU WILL

I knew something was up, I was never stupid, your mum was always on her phone playing that game, and he at work was always on his phone playing that game, they would both talk to me about how they beat each other; I was beginning to get worried now. I was at work providing everything for your mum and yourself, whilst she didn't care about looking after you or me and probably trying to cook for me because I was working late etc.... instead she wanted another guy, she was putting all her time and effort into that rather than doing what she should for her own family. I was always going to be suspicious, especially with what I knew of your mum, but what could I say or do, you was young, I had just moved away from my family, any sort of action from me and I would lose everything, I had no option but to remain silent, and go along with the ride by acting dumb and like nothing bothered me.

It got to the stage where I got annoyed, she never got off that stupid phone, so I snatched her phone from her hands whilst we both laid in bed one evening, she tried to wrestle it off me, in fact I had to run out the room and close the door on her so she couldn't get to me whilst I went through her messages. Just like every time she gets caught in the act, or the truth comes out, your mum got scared. I knew she was up to something, my gut feelings were and are never wrong.

What I saw was proof, she was blatantly flirting with this guy, I wanted to chuck your mum out the house there and then, I felt sick, I felt worthless, I was always taking you to your nene in the mornings, to be honest it was always me that got you ready in the mornings as well, I worked endless hours, picked you up, came home, cooked, washed, cleaned, whilst all your mum did was flirt with this so called friend of mine, but then again god knows how many other guys she was talking to. If I didn't have you the decision of throwing your mum into the streets back where she belongs would not have been a problem. However my problem, and the way I think, is that this so called person was the mother of my child, and no matter how selfish or morally wrong she was or is, I'm not like that, I have respect, even though she really didn't deserve any from me.

I just said to her, don't fall for his trap, this is what he does, and he is doing it to you, your mum said she knew what she was doing, a month later my family broke up, she knew what she was doing, she got what she wanted and no matter how much she will try and put the blame on my so called worker, I will always hold her responsible for her own actions.

REMEMBER THAT THE GRASS IS GREENER, WHERE YOU WATER IT

Before all this was confirmed that your mum and I had finished, before I knew all the evidence, and before I was clued up on it all, it got to the stage I had to do something about the life of our family or shall I say life as a family because you was part of our life. I knew how hard I was working, but I had to, I still put you and your mum first, but I had a plan. Early January once Christmas was out the way, and before your second birthday I was to propose to your mum. It obviously didn't work, money to me meant nothing as I know it can't and won't bring you any sort of happiness, yes it can give you an easy life, but all money will do is attract to you fake people who don't want you for who you are but for what you are worth. I spent near one thousand five hundred pounds on a ring, your ungrateful mum always wanted the expensive ring, I took her to the Hilton hotel, Michelin star food, but yet it didn't work. She did at one stage say yes, but I think it was more to do with the fact she was looking at the ring at the time she said yes. However I hand on heart believe her own guilt got in the way of us working, I believe everything she has done to me, all the secrets she holds, she knew there was no way she could ever be with me. Knowing how many secrets she had in the past, maybe these spun in her head, and if I and she were ever going to work, she would need to come clean, but as I said your mum won't ever admit she is wrong. So with this thinking she couldn't see a future with us, because she would always be living a lie. It was either that or the other guy was seriously on her mind constantly, all she did that evening at the hotel was sit on her phone pretending to search the internet for random things, clearly I was always in a losing battle.

MONEY WILL ONLY ATTRACT FAKE PEOPLE

When I questioned what she was doing, the response I got was that I should know what she is like and I should leave her alone, in other words, I'm talking and getting it on with a mate of yours, so don't you dare get in the way. I was none the wiser at that moment of time but it was all confirmed the day before your second birthday.

I was upstairs putting you to bed, your mum was downstairs on her phone, I knew she was up to something, especially when I saw a message she left on this guy's Facebook calling him the king. That's at the moment I thought I need to spy. I always knew your mum's Facebook password, when your suspicious of people you always have your ways, I was able to get this from a day that she left her mobile at home when she went work, this was when we had recently moved into the new house, and when we had come back from holiday. If I'm being honest it's at that very moment when I went through your mum's phone that I lost any trust in your mum, I would never trust your mum from that moment on. It's a shame I found out when I did, if only I didn't move into a new house, if only I didn't move away from my friends and family. When I checked your mum's Facebook, she was messaging some other guy telling him that she had a trampoline in the new house and they could jump up and down on it together, did I forget to mention naked? Amongst the other stuff I read, I've just left it clean for your sake. Also within her text messages she was flirting with her new boss and also a near if not older than fifty year old guy she was working with. Recently when I have questioned that she flirted and had relationships with these guys, which I will put my hand on my heart, and tell you I believe that she has, she denied it, she use to deny it by swearing on your life, how it winds me up when she does that to get herself out of trouble, especially when I know the truth. But does this not show you just exactly how nothing means more to your mum then herself? Not even you, her own child is safe when it comes to protecting herself.

Now you might be thinking your mum may never try it with a fifty year old guy, nor would she try it with her boss or even get involved with him, especially when he had a partner, and maybe even a kid, but that I'm not too sure of. I even found out that before I met your mum, and possibly even whilst I was with your mum, she had a fling with her old boss within the store I first met your mum in. This guy again was probably in his mid forties, and I know he was married and he had kids. But as I got to know your mum better with time, these sorts of facts didn't surprise me; she didn't care about her own daughter's family, why should she care about another man's kid's family? After all I know all your mum cares about is herself and no one else.

I WAS GULLIBLE

I did question your mum on the Facebook trampoline conversation that I found and read, but the messages were a couple of months old and I knew that from when I read them. She said she realised she made a mistake and stopped. I believed your mum, was I being gullible? I think I was. My wanting of you having a proper life was too high on the agenda, so I turned a blind eye. As for the text messages, that's something I'd keep a close eye on, but never spoke out as I had no evidence until our family had broke down.

Immediately when I saw your mum message my so called work mate calling him a king on his Facebook page, I signed into your mums facebook account from my phone, and I saw all the conversation in private messages develop right in front of my eyes. Your mum and this guy flirting away, making me look like a fool, making me look so small and worthless. My so called work mate was telling her that I would clock on and realise and that she was taking a big risk leaving that message on his Facebook wall, her reply not in so many words were that I was stupid and I would never realise or question her. I gave your mum a home, a family, a life that most girls would have wanted with me; I gave this guy a job, a position in which he could progress, a reputation which was priceless. I didn't deserve what these two people were doing to me; you didn't deserve what was going to happen.

PEOPLE MAKE PEOPLE ANGRY WITH SELF INFLICTED ACTIONS

I was fuming, but I still kept my nerve and put you to bed first before I went downstairs and threw my phone at your mum's lap. Your mum went white and believe me that's not an expression, she went white, she had been caught red handed. She swore on your life nothing had happened, but the Wednesday that week, I was to cook some food that we were to trial out for your birthday party, she text me last minute to say she was going out for dinner with work, I went mad, all she had to say was that she was sorry, but thinking back now, it made sense. He was off on a Wednesday; she obviously went to see him after she finished work.

The anger as I write this is too much, and writing this proves to me how much I can't ever be with your mum again. As you will read there are times I thought maybe we should have, and even thought for your sake I should, but the fact is, I'm hurt because your mum ruined both our lives, but more so you, because you will never have that family life you deserve.

I just need to let you know again before you read anymore, because you may feel that I'm upset and that my life was ruined by you, some of the things I will say will make you realise I was and am sad, will make you realise how much I hate my life or shall I say hated life. But believe me, you're my saviour in this entire saga. I love you, and this is why I'm always here and there for you, You will never ever have to face things alone, because I am going to make sure you have the life of a princess that you deserve, because you're daddy's little princess.

YOU'RE MY SAVIOUR IN ALL THIS

My supervisor at work, someone who is like a brother to me within my workplace, told me in confidence that I should be careful, he knew that our work colleague and your mum was playing behind my back, he had apparently confided in him, but when I questioned your mum, she swore on your life she never met him, and even more swore again nothing had happened between the two of them, and everything was in my head. I know how hard it must be for you to hear how often your mum swears on your life, especially when you know she does it to protect herself, but believe me the more she swore on your life the more it angered me, how dare she put my daughter's life in danger by lying to protect herself.

However things began to take place, it all begun to make sense, your mum for a week was finding silly little things to break up with me, I flicked a woolly hat in her face jokingly to tell her to listen to me because she was ignoring me, the reaction I got was, "I can't believe you have hit me, we're finished"

IF I EVER HIT YOUR MUM, BELIEVE ME SHE'LL NEVER EVER GET BACK UP

I would never hit your mum, even though there have been stages that I could have, no woman on this earth would be this blind to see how lucky they are or shall I say were to get everything and anything, without putting anything in to the relationship.

Anyway the day came, your mum said she had enough, I told her some home truths, she was unhappy, I was unhappy, I told her that I had opportunities to flirt and cheat with other girls and I never, because I valued my family more, she asked for examples, I told her the truth, I had a customer who used to come in and flirt, she asked to meet me once, I said no because I had a family, I never saw the girl ever again after that, she never did her shopping from my store ever again. There's been girls on rare occasions I've gone out, like a barmaid who blatantly flirted or even random girls who would just bump into me, believe me if I had intentions I would and could have, and believe me even more, if I had set out to cheat, I know I could find anyone I wanted to. I actually believe maybe your mum's thinking was that I can't find anyone, so I shall stay loyal for that reason alone. Maybe your nanny's comments echoed in her own ears, your nanny used to tell me I was lucky to have your mum, maybe your mum literally thought that was true, but in fact as the relationship got older, it was obvious and clear that in fact it was your mum who was the lucky one to have me.

IT WAS YOUR MUM WHO WAS LUCKY TO HAVE ME

Your mum and this so called friend of mine was beginning to play mind games with me and this is what made me more and more angry.

Before it was confirmed that they were seeing each other, and slowly I was realising that they were playing behind my back. This so called friend at Christmas would ask me what sort of things your mum liked, what sort of handbags she liked because apparently he could get them cheap if I wanted any. I didn't think of it at the time, but he knew I had already brought your mum a Tiffany bracelet because she wanted it, but maybe he was asking because he wanted to buy her the gifts and what better brownie points but to buy her a make and style that she liked? Your mum has always been about appearance, always wanting the top of the range stuff. For example, when we moved in to the new house, a standard ninety nine pence slotted spoon would not do, it had to be the sixty quid set of six, or a normal bath mat that would cost about ten quid would not do, how dare I even think about buying something of this calibre, yet again it had to be the Egyptian cotton mat that cost about seventy quid. But you know what? I didn't care, if it made your mum happy, I did it. This is why I also feel your mum began to look elsewhere, My money began to dry up, I spent over thirty grand in moving and buying new stuff for the house, I wasn't flashing the money about the way I was, I had to be careful, I didn't want to waste it all, I wanted to save some for you.

DON'T EVER LET MONEY BE THE FOCUS OF YOUR LIFE

Your mum was getting architects to draw up plans on how to extend the house, even after I told her I couldn't afford it yet, I had to pay the bills, she wouldn't pay a penny for anything, all your mum would do is pay me two hundred quid a month towards all the bills that exceeded one thousand three hundred pounds.

I have no idea what your mum did with her money, she got a decent wage, she really didn't have much to spend out, she even took all your child support allowance, not once did I ever ask for this, yet she paid for nothing, not even food for you.

Your mum thinks she is clever, but I spot and know everything and just because I don't speak out it's because I have respect for myself and I don't want you to get in the middle of everything.

Back to the mind games that were being played with me, on one specific day before I realised your mum and my relationship was over, I thought I'd try and win her back. The ring, the hotel, the meal, I knew that didn't work. I couldn't understand why? Although she did tell me if I brought her a new car she would come back. I never gave in to that request, there's no way I was spending over twenty grand to keep her in a family she should have wanted to be with. It was already me that had put my name on some finance agreement which got her the car she had then, it makes me angry, I made your mum, I did everything and beyond to what she wanted, she never ever thought of me, or you, it was always her.

What puzzled me more was a couple of months prior she was telling all my family at your cousin's birthday party how she wanted to marry me and wanted more kids with me, either way I thought I'd just jog her memory to make her realise what she was doing, I thought I'd send your mum fifty red roses to her work with a message that stated everything we had been through from the moment we first met. It didn't work, I got confirmation by the flower people it had been delivered, so I watched my phone, but I didn't get the call. Instead my so called friend's phone rang whilst we both worked; he looked at his phone and went outside into the service yard to pretend he was getting some stock from the outside container. I watched from a distance, I slowly made my way to the back only to see him hang up once he saw me. I had to question him, and I did, I told him to show me his phone, told him to be a man and show me who he was speaking to.

YOU ONLY HIDE WRONG DOINGS, AND LIE TO COVER IT UP

He never showed me, he was never man enough to tell me to my face what he did, instead he told me I was breaking his privacy, and I apparently knew that he wouldn't do anything bad to me because he respected me, he also told me I was going crazy thinking him and your mum were getting it on behind my back. I was going crazy; I needed answers, I nearly snatched his phone out of his hand. About ten minutes later your mum phones me, not the conversation I was expecting, I told her that I got into a confrontation with this guy, but your mum slipped up, I never once told her what happened, but your mum said "you really shouldn't snatch his phone out of his hand" I never once mentioned a phone to your mum, how did she know? I tell you how she knew, she phoned him or he phoned her.

Your mum kept telling me that I had, in our conversation, told her I tried to snatch his phone out his hands, and that I was going insane for not remembering it, it's always me going crazy when your mum don't want the truth out, but she yet again swore on your life that I had told her this, but I promise you on everything I am to you, I never, I was more clued up then you or anyone may think.

Your mum didn't come home to stay after that for about five days, she wanted a break, well time alone with this guy, and she even told me not to phone her, no matter what. No matter what! I was looking after her child, I had work, but under no circumstances was I allowed to call her, another example of what your mum's priorities in life are. However this absence of your mum is where the bond between daddy and daughter amazingly began to grow stronger than it already was, you were forced to trust me even more then you already did, so your mum should always remember whenever you cry or call for me, it's her fault and no one else's and she should allow what you want.

YOU WILL ALWAYS BE A DADDY'S GIRL

I had to get the truth out of this guy and your mum, I said I had friends in the police force which I do, and that one was to source and forward messages to and from your mum's phone so I could find the scumbag who ruined my family. They both got scared, this apparent mate of mine now came to tell me everything, and apparently your mum and he had met up twice prior to this whole ordeal. This is how honest and trustworthy your mum is, she swore on your life not once, not twice but over and over again that she never met him, she swore on your life that it was never him.

I can't tell you how hurt I am that anyone can swear on my daughter's life and lie to protect themselves. If it was not your mum swearing on your life, I promise I would have hurt them, but I always feel that if I hurt your mum in anyway, in some strange way I'll end up hurting you, and maybe you'll never ever forgive me for it. With all this in mind, we are talking about your mum, this is a woman who should put herself in harm's way to protect you, not put you in harm's way to protect herself. I promise you every time I think of this, my blood boils, I get angry and extremely emotional, and I hate your mum for that. She always used you to get what she wants, and she knew you were my precious little thing and she used that against me all the time.

Just so you can get a slight insight into the life I was living at that time, your mum had disappeared to another life she wanted, I still had work, I had to look after you. Whilst at work I had to work with this guy, every time I looked in his face I wanted to hit him, make him pay, maybe I should have let my family beat him up. On the day it was confirmed that he had been the reason to my daughter not having a family, my family went after him, and he would have been injured if I didn't stop it. This is one thing you will realise as you get older, the support and the togetherness within our family is second to none. It may seem at times that we don't get on, maybe at times it seems we hate each other, but our bond as a family is good, we sometimes if not all the time tell it to your face. We may be loud, but we are proud of who we are.

MY PROBLEMS WERE IN MY FACE WHERE EVER I WENT

I had to see and work with this guy for months, I was leaving my house where I had problems, work should have been a good thing as it should have helped me get away from my issues, but I was unable to do this, that so called mate of mine was in my face, in my mind I had thoughts of him boasting to my staff what he was doing, my personal life was everywhere. It was crazy, my personal life was at work and it was causing me so much grief, I couldn't get away from it from anywhere, my mind and my thoughts were spinning around nonstop. I had to push for this guy's promotion just to get him out of the store I was in, because without a promotion I could not get him out my store, I was told by my boss I had to deal with it, and if I did anything unprofessional then I would be dealt with accordingly.

I knew deep down he wasn't ready for his promotion, but I needed him out. One thing I will say, and that one thing is for sure, I never forget, whether that means I do something about it in the future or not, is up to me.

As for your mum, I couldn't live with her, she was in my face and she was rubbing it in. Just imagine everything you have sacrificed, I left my family, friends, I put strain on my day because I was adding an hour and a half on to my journey to and from work, also imagine the tiredness I had from doing everything for your mum as well as for you, add the long hours at work, add the extra money I had to pay on bills then imagine coming home and hearing your mum deliberately talking on the phone to this guy so I could hear her conversations. I had to pretend it didn't bother me, had to try and force myself to smile, but I couldn't, especially when she started saying love you on the phone to him. I was like really? After two weeks you love this guy, guess what your mum's response was? I love him more than I ever loved you, but this is the same person who a few months prior still wanted everything, who still wanted the family that I wanted. Deep inside I knew how this guy operated and I genuinely thought that he had played on your mum's mind and had her turned against me, especially when she didn't believe a word I said. I told your mum what I knew, the truths of how he used to throw cans of beans at this girl he dated at work, how she use to moan to me that he could turn violent and possibly hit her, but your mum chose not to believe me, instead she believed him. It's funny really because everything I told your mum was true but she chose to think I lied. As for your mum, all she ever did was lie and I chose to ignore and not argue, what sort of person did she think I was? What sort or relationship did we really have? Never once did she ever listen to me, it was always about her.

SOME PEOPLE DON'T KNOW THE TRUE MEANING OF LOVE

It hurt me big time hearing your mum saying she loved him more; did I really waste my time with your mum? Was it wise of me to put my health at risk for your mum? Because I wasn't eating properly, wasn't eating at the right times and was rushing eating my food with foods that weren't good for me. I had little exercise, on top of that no rest, on the other hand, your mum had time for everything, ate three times a day, exercised on her ski machine, had time to herself in the mornings, a hour lunch as well as time to herself in the afternoons, why did I waste my time? Well I didn't really waste it, because most of it was for you. I just hate that your mum was around to experience a life that she didn't deserve.

In saying that statement, a life she didn't deserve, it makes me think, who gave your mum the platform to have what she has? Who gave her the opportunity to study? Who gave her the opportunity to work full time and have a career? Most mums stay at home, but I knew your mum was young, I thought she wanted that career because that's what she told me. I didn't want her to feel she had wasted her life, a statement she threw in my face. I was told on numerous occasions that she was too young and that she hasn't lived, and that she wants to do this and that with her friends and that she wants to go out and live her life. I wish I'd listened to my family when I got with your mum, they did warn me saying she was too young, and that she would give me issues. I chose to believe your mum thinking she would prove them wrong and that I knew best, maybe a lesson for you in the future from which you can learn, listen to the people who only have your best interest at heart.

I gave your mum the time to study, I gave her everything she wanted, maybe I gave her too much, gave her too much independence because it really did get to her head and build her ego knowing I'd do anything and everything.

Just like the week before we split, she knew we were going to split up, but she wanted to pay off her credit card that she built up, so she made me pay over a grand to do this, so she could apply for a loan to get a new car, another image and ego boosting materialistic thing your mum didn't need. Deep in her head your mum knew she never wanted me, why did she do this? Because it's always about your mum, always what she wants, and most of the time it's to do with money. To be honest, I actually feel any guy can have your mum if they wave money in front of her eyes, she did tell me once she slept with a guy who gave her two hundred quid to do so, no comment there I guess.

I WAS BEING USED AGAIN

I was now at a point that I was in a bad state with your mum, do I agree with what I am about to say to you? No I don't, but would I do it again?

Yes I would. Your mum was being a pain, making my life as awkward as she could, she parked her car in front of my car as she normally did, blocking me in the drive way, she well and truly knew I had to go work early, and I had to take you to your nene's. She wouldn't move the car even after I asked nicely. I warned her if I had to move her car that I would move it miles away to teach her a lesson, but because your mum's cousin stayed the night as they went to a concert the night before, I believe she wanted to prove a point to her cousin. A point that showed she had authority, but to me at that moment in time, she began to look like the worst spoilt little brat I'd ever seen in my whole entire life.

I was in no mood to play games, I warned her several times, and I did what I said, she didn't like it, she demanded I tell her where I put the car, I didn't that's when she started throwing stones and rocks at my car, I went mad told her to stop. As I picked you up to put you in the car, she started punching the back of my head. What was I supposed to do? I have so much anger in me, most guys in my position I swear would have hit your mum there and then, she would have deserved it, I don't agree with hitting women, but she was really crossing the line now. I did what came as my first instinct, I put you down, I couldn't believe she was hitting me whilst you were in my hands, I turned around and I went mad, I shouted, asking what she was playing at, and to leave me alone, that's when I held her hands because she was now aiming her punches towards my face, I pinned her on the stairs and shouted directly in her face, I really wanted to hit your mum, I really did, my blood was boiling, the back of my head was hurting from her punches, but I'm a man and I don't hit women so I didn't, instead I did what I could, and I did what came to my mind first, I spat in her face, and told her that's what I thought of her.

ALL I COULD DO WAS SPIT

I'm glad for your nanny realising your mum had to leave the house, I was continuously putting pressure on your mum, asking her to leave, she wasn't pulling her weight around, was paying no bills, her contribution to the house was minimal I could do it without her. I regret putting her name on the mortgage, my mum, your nene gave me money, a large amount when I originally brought my house in Chingford, but because I thought your mum was the one, I had no doubts in allowing her name to go on the mortgage. This is probably the worst mistake I've ever made, my mum's money, my dad, may his soul be resting, worked hard to leave me that money, just like I work hard for you, and if I die I know I've left something behind for you, your mum is not entitled to anything, all your mum has paid towards bills since us moving way back in June 2012 is no more than one thousand two hundred pounds, that's absolutely nothing in my eyes.

I wanted this so called mate of mine to live up to what he did, he wanted my family, he should go and buy a place with your mum, go show how much he wanted my family in particular this so called woman who to me is unfortunately your mum. What would wind me up even more was that she was looking for places near where he lived, this made me livid, I moved away from that area because she wanted to move nearer her family, she wanted you to grow up out of London, what was she doing? If anything he should have been looking for a place near Romford. Your mum said I was being unreasonable, in my eyes, your mum screwed my life up for her own gain, and was again throwing me in the gutter by saying "screw you, I'm moving back in to London with my new boyfriend". Anyways I continuously put pressure on your mum to get a place, and I think your nanny realised your mum was making a big mistake, she told me that she and your grandpa was very disappointed with what your mum had done, so she took her in, maybe not for your mums sake but mainly for yours, at least I'd know you were safe, I would have the thought knowing if your mum was being herself and allowing you to just do what you want, and she would just get carried away with her life, then I know your nanny wouldn't allow it or at worst it be your nanny that looked after you.

We worked on a basis of one week I had you Sunday, Monday, Tuesday, Friday Saturday then the following week I had you Wednesday Thursday, It did work well, but the days I didn't see you were torture, not knowing you were safe, not knowing what you were doing was hurting me. I phoned you up one evening to say good night because I was feeling really low, as soon as you heard my voice and we started talking, you started crying, saying you wanted daddy, I put the phone down with you crying in the background for me; your mum told me I was making things worse by phoning you and not to do so any more. I wasn't like your mum and I never will be, I can't go days or weeks without seeing you, it really is hard for me not to know how safe you are, because I need to be there for you when you call for me, because that's what you are used to. You're used to daddy being there when you need him, you know of nothing else. Just the thought of you calling for me, and me not being able to hear your call, and me not being able to come to you really upsets me and distresses me, because you're having to learn something you don't want to learn and get used to. You're used to daddy being by your side at all times, that's what you have grown up with since you were born; it's just not fair on you to have that taken away. Just like me, you're faultless in all of the drama that has been created.

YOU WILL ONLY EVER HAVE ONE DAD

The hardest thing for me to ever accept and will until the day that I die will be the thought of another man holding your hand, buying you gifts, cuddling you, or just doing things that I should be doing with you. It's rather ironic that I say this, because about a year before me and your mum split, I wrote a script, it was a film that I titled "My Two Girls" your mum started to read the story, but she never finished it, when I asked why, all she said was that the whole idea of the story and my thinking was morbid, to me the story was romantic and showed my love towards both of you. Looking back at it now, maybe there was other things in your mums agenda like other guys that stopped your mum reading the story, maybe guilt got in her way. It was a story about me, a man who was dying but kept it quite, I told a lie saying that I loved someone else and went to live with them, but the truth was that he left to die alone; the thoughts behind this were because I lost my dad when I was thirteen. My dad got terminally ill when I was eleven, I saw things that scared me and probably will for the rest of my whole life, I saw my family struggle, and if I'm honest my family has never recovered from it. So the story I wrote was based on me not wanting to leave that scar, that pain behind so your mum could move on without regret, and hope to find someone who you could call dad, because to me, having a normal childhood is the most important thing, and I will strive to give that to you as a single dad in real life, it will be hard, but you know what, I promise I will be the best dad in the world.

I SEEMED TO HAVE LIVED THAT SCRIPT IN REAL LIFE

The script I wrote shows me as a spirit, hurting not being able to rest in peace as you don't know who I am, who your real dad was. What pains me more is when I see another man in my shoes, not being able to walk you down the aisle, not being there for you, but also the hardest thing, you not knowing who I was. The story revolves around a wish I left with my brother, a wish that once your mum was happy, for her to be told the truth to clear my name of bad doing, but also for you to know how much your dad really loved you. That's the basis of the story and what things happen for you to find out, and also for you to get the truth out your mum as she is in denial. When I wrote that script, every word was true about your mum; however they are all false now, as for you, every word is stronger than when I originally wrote it.

So imagine how I felt after writing that story, knowing your mum wanted you to meet this guy, my so called mate, a guy in which she loved more than anything in the world. I told her to wait, but I know she didn't, I shouted and screamed at your mum, told her to let me get used to the idea, I told her not to confuse you, she said she wouldn't, but I know deep down she did, because you would come up to me, holding a chocolate telling me his name and telling me he brought it for you, but your mum always denied he did, she played on this whole mental struggle I had, and I know she enjoyed seeing me crumble, she enjoyed doing it to me. There's times when she picked you up from me, she would make sure she would give you a magazine, and deliberately tell you in front of me that he brought it for you, why would she do this? Why when she knew that I was crumbling and fading with the fact that some other man was getting his claws into my daughter.

YOU TOLD ME EVERYTHING

There was a time, I can't remember why, I had to go into your mums car to get something, situated on the back seat was a fleece, a work fleece with the company I work for's logo on it, you were in my hand because that's the way you are, always wanting me where ever I go. As soon as you saw the fleece, you made sure to tell me that it was this guy's fleece. I know you don't lie, when I use my laptop, you would tell me that mummy spoke to him on the laptop, obviously through Skype, and you told me she did this when she was putting you to bed. It hurts because to me putting you to bed should just be special, instead other things were more important then you, but it also hurts that again your mum swore you didn't meet him, and everything you were saying to me was random and that you was lying to me. A child your age would never know how to lie, you may understand the grasp of joking, but a Child's mentality wouldn't be developed enough to understand that this is the sort of thing or things to lie about. I don't think the things you said to me were random, because you would even tell me that mummy would show you photos of him on mummy's phone. I need to say this now, I never once probed you to tell me any details, I never wanted to know, all I wanted was to forget everything, blank everything, and imagine nothing was happening, every day I wished I would just wake up and everything I had felt was a bad nightmare. I felt sick to think about it and what was happening to us, I didn't want more stress or random grief plus it wouldn't be fair on you if I did question you, at the age you were and are now any questions to anything away from having fun and learning is not what you need, you need to live a normal toddler life. But you told me everything in random games or conversations that we had and played, none of this ever helped me, my own daughter telling me of the other half of your life I didn't want to hear or know about.

DON'T BE ASHAMED TO CRY

Your mum became a child, she really did. The more childish she became, the more I hated her because the strain and pressure she was putting on both you and me, was just too much to handle. I actually began to get very angry with people around me, I started to have a short fuse, my patience was fading and my anger was being aimed at people close to me like my mum; I know I had a problem, because I would just cry at home alone. Don't get me wrong the tears were never over your mum, a lot of the tears were for you, but most were because I was stuck in this hole, not being able to move on with my life, not being able to do anything I wanted, instead it was your mum that had gone to get on with her life, but it was still her that was dictating my life. It really hurt me hard thinking that I had done nothing wrong, I had done everything she wanted, I had done what every girl in the world wants from a guy, both as a partner and the father of their child, but it wasn't enough for your mum. I can't explain how hard it is to accept that, I sometimes wish I was actually a bad guy, done things wrong, done things to deserve what I was going through, because then I believe I would have answers to my failures.

THE PRESSURES OF LIFE CAN AND WILL ADD UP IN TIME

I tried to get my life back on track, and your mum was going out with my work colleague, he had now been transferred to another store, that made my life a lot easier than it had been, but believe me, although I say easier, it was far from easy, it was still as hard as anything I've ever had to deal with. Something about my work that needs to be said is that my work life is stressful, I'm a store manager in charge of a mini supermarket, as well as trying to keep the store standards and service to a high standard, I have to ensure that my staff are fully trained and are working towards the set targets. I don't work a normal nine to five job like your mum, I don't have weekends off like your mum, I have to be flexible with what days and hours I can work, I have to commit to my job, dedication has to be without a doubt a key attribute to the job I do. Between you and my job, I had no other thoughts or interests, and although my job was hectic, it may have been the other reason away from you that kept me from actually going crazy because it allowed me to be busy and not think things through all the time.

With what your mum had done, she made me feel embarrassed at work, when reality sunk in, I was around people who all knew my private life, were they laughing behind my back? I will never know, but if I did catch them laughing, I wouldn't feel bad for me, it was you and always will be you that I get upset about when I think about it. You have a broken home; you can't have the best of both worlds, but in fact in the future you will have to decide on what you want; a decision that you should never have to make in my eyes.

MY LOWEST POINT WITH YOU

With all this pressure going on in my life, and your mum being the main cause, I did something I will never forgive myself for, and believe me I am crying my eyes out as I write this. I was in a bad place, your mum was being unfair, your mum's mind games were getting too much and it was always about your mum, I couldn't understand why, it should have been all about you. I wanted some time alone as well, maybe to grieve, maybe to accept what had happened had actually happened, I wanted to go out and let my hair down, I was tired of doing the same thing every day, instead your mum kept throwing at me that it's all my fault, it's the life I chose to live, but I never chose to live away from my family and friends and become financially insecure because I tried to do what was best for your mum and you.

One day, a day that I had you, you wouldn't stop moaning, you were tired, you were restless, and I just shouted at you to be quiet, I told you to sit down for just five minutes, you wouldn't sleep, the house was a mess, I had problems at work, your mum kept telling me she was going to spend the whole of bank holiday with you and my so called work colleague, I was hungry, and it all got to me. I shouted so much you got frightened, I saw the fear in your eyes, I saw the tears flow down your cheeks, and it was that moment I realised what I did was wrong, I tried to give you a cuddle, but you didn't want one, that's the first time you never wanted one from me, and what hurt more is that when you were crying you were calling for and saying you wanted mummy, you had never said that before to me whilst in my presence, it was always about you and me. What did I do? What was I becoming? I'm so sorry, I really am, that night I put you to sleep, and I promise that night I didn't sleep a wink thinking of what I did, I gave you a cuddle and a kiss on the forehead as you slept and I whispered and promised never to shout at you again like that, your mum was not worth the bother of me losing my relationship with you. I gathered that, but everything was getting on top of me, the previous day when you were with your mum, I got lonely and annoyed, and with the fact that I was missing you, I threw the coffee tables against the walls and floors of the living room to let my anger out. That moment you called for your mum, just got me thinking, I and in particular you don't deserve the grief that was going on, I realised you must have been so confused, I wanted to make things easier for you, not more difficult. The next morning you woke up, I asked you for a cuddle, hoping I would get one, and I did, that cuddle meant so much to me. As I held you I held you tightly, I said sorry, told I would never shout at you again, gave you a kiss, and that was the end of that. As I said no woman who ever they may be which includes your mum, and no other person in this world whoever they are is going to break my bond with you, ever. When I make promises I keep to them, and that's a promise that I will always keep.

I PROMISE YOU I'LL ALWAYS BE THERE

It really played on me what happened, and I searched online for help, someone to talk to, I had so much anger, so much frustration within me, I needed to let it out. Your hala did try and help, and out of anyone she helped me the most in terms of speaking to me and listening to me. Your nene was always there helping me out by looking after you and with money, your uncle was your uncle, I wouldn't ask him to be anything else, he was supportive in his own way, my niece sent me a touching text telling me how much she loved me, as did my nephew, but it was your hala who talked to me. I needed to talk to someone and share my feelings and it did help, but with your hala and anyone else that knew me, there was only so far I could go, only so much I would open up to. I had to remain and show your hala I was strong, after all she was my sister. This is the moment I searched online for help. After several hours of searching for help, I must admit it was a struggle, as all I wanted to do was speak to someone online there and then, but there was no sort of service available, most required money and I was dubious of this. I found one guy who I believe lived in Australia, I believe it was called the parachute programme or something, I added him on facebook, and I spoke to him for about half hour on Skype but due to our time differences and my commitments it was hard to talk to him. Although I didn't speak to him much, he did say one thing that stuck in my mind, I said I was crying for you, but he told me the tears I shed were from my eyes and not yours, those words have stuck in my head, and are so true as I write this now because although you feel my love, I'm thankful you can't feel all my pain.

After searching again online I eventually found the phone number to the Samaritans, they seemed the only help around, I phoned twice, I said hello on both occasions but I put the phone down immediately after, in a strange way I was disappointed I never got a phone call back to ask if everything was ok, or ask if someone had called. I know I desperately needed help, but I didn't know how to ask for it without looking like a fool. As silly as this may sound, I wanted someone to see I needed help rather than me say I needed help.

I NEEDED SOMEONE TO SEE I NEEDED HELP, HOW COULD NO ONE SEE?

My mind was all over the place, I knew of this because mentally I was struggling in coping with my everyday tasks, I really needed to talk to someone, someone who didn't know me, I didn't want to talk to someone who would know who I was and knew what had happened. I just wanted someone to listen to me, and not give me answers to why things went wrong. All I got from my family was that if I had listened to them then I wouldn't be in this mess I was in or constantly giving me recommendations on what to do. I just wanted someone that wouldn't judge who I was, someone who would just listen. It's only when something like this happens to you when you realise you're all alone in this world, the people you have around you no matter how much good intention they have towards you, are not the people you want help from.

The internet seemed to be the only tool I had available for the help I was after, it was the only discreet aid I possibly could have without anyone and everyone knowing I needed help. Again I searched the internet and this is when I found a therapist based in Walthamstow that I would go and see. I decided against going to the doctor or the NHS, I felt like if I did it would feel like I had been defeated. I didn't want them to know what was happening to me, I felt all they would do is feed me with pills and make me out to be crazy, and I somewhat thought if this is what they did then this would give ammunition to people in particular to your mum to falsely show I was not a good dad. Maybe I was scared that the authorities would think I am not able to be a dad to you and ultimately lose you, this is why I went private, and this is why I kept everything private from everyone, I didn't want anyone to see I was weak and I was struggling in the inside, instead everyone began to see a fake me and they all believed it, I seemed to be indestructible to the people looking at me, but believe me no one in this world is indestructible, everyone can be knocked down somehow. One thing is for sure and too many people in this world do it, is that people judge people on things they don't know, a statement which I truly believe in is that you should "never judge a book by its cover" and even when you have read the story, again I am sure there are many people who won't understand it first time.

NEVER JUDGE A BOOK BY ITS COVER

I went private and I have no idea even if this lady I was going to see was qualified, I had to pay forty pounds a session, its money I couldn't afford, but it made me feel better even after the first session. The lady I was speaking to realised and understood everything, she understood that everything I was doing was for you, realised that I was a fool for ever loving and trusting your mum, a fool for doing everything for your mum at her request. I could see in her eyes and her posture towards me that she felt sorry for me, and in a way, maybe that's what I needed, in the real life I'm full of smiles to everyone, always joking, trying to keep a brave face, I never let my guard down, I never let anyone see how weak I am, never let anyone see I need help, I'm the guy everyone looks up to, I'm the guy everyone goes to for help, or the guy everyone goes to, to get a laugh.

Away from your nene, your uncle, auntie, and hala, no one really knew the truth, and even then, the ones that thought they knew everything, even they only knew a fraction of the truth. My close family saw me cry, they saw my life crumble, they told me to stand up and fight, told me to not give up, told me to not just stop and let my life waste away. But what was I supposed to do? I felt I had no one. Why do I say this? Because when all this was happening, I knew everyone knew about my problems and difficulties, and it upsets me that I didn't get one call or even a text from the people I thought were close to me, instead they just ignored me. My closest cousin, someone who I genuinely thought would be by my corner, this was not just a cousin to me, he was also my best friend, my cousin was the one I grew up with when we were kids. He is the earliest memory I have as a child, he seemed to have disappeared in my hour of need, not one message from him to say "here for you" that's all I needed, I wouldn't have confided or talked to him, that's not my style, I just needed to know I had support, and it's because of this I now feel I've lost that closeness and maybe trust I thought I had with him, that closeness and trust that we built by growing up together as little kids.

I didn't have many friends left, to be honest I can count my friends on one hand, you see they all disappeared gradually when I chose your mum over them. The couple that I had remaining may have thought they were close, but they too were nowhere in sight, I was all alone, and I couldn't and wouldn't rely on my close family to help me anymore then they were. My best mate, he was around for me, we went out at nights when I didn't have you, and believe me this was good for me, but he never knew the truth, didn't know exactly what your mum was doing, but I needed someone who didn't know anything just as much as someone that knew everything, that is how confusing my life got.

DON'T EVER USE AN INNOCENT PERSON AS A REASON TO GET WHAT YOU WANT

I tried to get my life back on track, and if I'm honest I was slowly making progress in doing that, work life was getting better and in regards to relationships I was getting in to the swing of things again, I had been on a few dates to see what sort of girls were out there, to see if I could gel with them, and there may have been relationships I was involved in that could and may have been something, but your mum put an end to these. The first was actually an old school friend, the chemistry between us was really good, our mental thoughts were similar, however she had a problem with your mum always phoning and texting me when I was with her.

Obviously you were with your mum at the times I would see her, maybe your mum felt vulnerable, maybe she felt jealous, but why on Gods earth would she text me messages like get me tampons? Or send me messages that you're not well and that she may take you to the hospital? I tell you why, your mum knew that I would do anything and everything for you, knowing you're not well is my worst nightmare, it will stop me doing anything at that moment of time, but on my quick return home I came home to see you and miraculously you had got better, not needing to go to the hospital. But now that I was home, your mum just said that she was going out and that I have to look after you, she immediately rushes out to see one of her boyfriends.

What this girl, my old school friend couldn't understand and one of a few reasons we could never get any further was the fact she couldn't accept you, couldn't accept that I was so involved in my daughter's life, yes your mum never made it easy, and I understand this because your mum was constantly on my back, and with the fact that your mum was living with your nanny a couple of streets away from where I lived, she was adamant that I would never be serious with another girl, all because if I love my daughter so much that I would do anything for my daughter's mother. To a degree at the time that was true but now, never, my daughter's mum can rot in the streets before I help her out, in fact id rather help endless homeless people before I even contemplate thinking about your mum, you'll understand more to why I say this as you read on. You may need to understand this as well, you see I have a big checklist now, a checklist that girls need to meet before I actually think they may be right for me, some will say that this is a stupid thing to have as it limits my choices, but my checklist will ensure we will never ever get hurt in the future, that's my priority now.

GET ME TAMPONS?

Everything is and will always be about your mum, I had no money because I was paying for bills, and I couldn't forever go out to restaurants, cinemas etc... This particular girl wanted reassurance that I wasn't playing behind her back with your mum, so she wanted to see where I lived, your mum knew I was going to bring her back to mine because I didn't want her to just pop round whilst I was entertaining. That night my phone never stopped ringing, the house phone never stopped, my old school friend walked out the house that night, and things were never the same between us ever again, the chemistry we had was lost and would never flame up again. The way I was feeling at that moment and the way I probably feel now is if people don't choose to trust me, I really don't want to fight for them, because I'm used to losing every time I fought for your mum.

I personally believe I am the most trustworthy person there is, but even I could see what your mum was doing was putting doubts in people's minds. What your mum was doing was so frustrating that it made me phone my ex co-worker to tell him what your mum was doing, and for him to sort out his girlfriend and for her to leave me alone, he said he would tell her to stop, but then as soon as I got off the phone, I began to think that your mum was making me play games in their relationship, I was getting involved in their relationship which I really didn't want to do. I began to think if I had a phone call from my girlfriends ex, telling me everything I just told him, I would really question that girl, in fact I would have left the relationship, so fair play to that guy, he stuck by your mum, for whatever reason it was, maybe it was guilt for what he did to me, but he stuck by her.

Your mum was getting in the way of my future, but not just mine, yours as well. I'm not like your mum, I won't show you or introduce you to just anybody, it needs and will take a lot for me to do that, the girl that does will have to win my trust, because that's something I believe I will struggle with, I truly believe I am never going to trust another girl ever again, it will take one hell of a special girl to convince me, and when they do, that's the girl I will marry.

HOW CAN I EVER TRUST ANYONE AGAIN?

Deep inside me, it was getting to me, it was ok for your mum to move on with her life, but poor old me had to wait, had to just sit and watch the world go by. My priority was you, it was no game to see who would get serious in a relationship first, but I believe your mum knew deep down if I did get serious with someone, what would she do? How would your mum live without my input, what would happen to you? After all its me that looks after you most, it's me you trust most, it's my family that help out every day, without me, she would lose you too, but being the man I am, being the dad I am to you, I still wanted your mum to be close to you, I wanted her to want you, but instead she was still more interested in her own life, and you really were second best to a lot of the things she did.

My life was taking a turn for the worst, my health was now deteriorating, my own family don't even know this, although your nene does know of the continuous moans I made about the pain in my back, it was her that kept saying and telling me to go to the doctors. I took a week off from work to go and have tests done, my back, in particular my lower back, located around where my kidneys were, was in severe pain, pain that would make me cry, and pain that would make me have to sit down or stand still when I was at work. My work was getting very difficult to do because of this condition, as I was always on my feet, always under pressure, I would have numerous, spontaneous occasions where I felt faint and always tired. I always put these symptoms down to tiredness, through being over worked, my personal life with you and your mum, as well as the stress from both my work and home life.

YOUR MUM PUT MY HEALTH AT RISK

It got to the stage I couldn't take anymore, I had to do something so I did, I actually went private for two reasons. Firstly I had been paying private care since I was seventeen and thought I should use it for once, but also because I wanted to get things done fast as I knew once I started work again, once I went back to work from my week off I just wouldn't have the time to get myself checked up and wouldn't be able to get the time off work again for follow up checks or tests, and the days that I did have off, I wanted to spend them with you as quality daddy and daughter time is what I look forward to most. I had quite a few tests done such as various blood tests, a scan, even a body fat test as well as others and on the second visit in that single week I got the results back; to be honest I wasn't surprised at what I was told, I had a slight high blood pressure which could be controlled without the need of tablets as long as I stay stress free that really wasn't anything to worry about, but the worrying thing was that I had slight inflamed kidneys, from what was put down to my lifestyle, tiredness, stress and because I wasn't drinking and eating the right things at the right times and in the right quantities. I was offered medication, but after I researched the name of the medication it warned me of side effects, one of which that stood out was that I could likely gain weight, I thought about it, but I declined. I knew that since I got together with your mum I had put weight on, all from not living that normal life, there was no way I wanted to gain more, the second and probably the most influential reason to why I declined was the simple reason that I couldn't afford to buy the medication, this wasn't an NHS prescription this was private and I couldn't afford what they wanted from me, they were to give me small quantities of tablets and then have to go for further check up's before they could give me more. Again, like I described I didn't have the time for any further checkups and I didn't have the funds for repeat prescriptions, I politely declined.

I'M LUCKY IT WASN'T TOO SERIOUS

I should be grateful that the medication wasn't that necessary, to be honest I've never been a guy to pop pills when I get a headache or pain here or there, I just don't see how they can work, in fact you may laugh here, but I can't even swallow those damn tablets, I either have to chew my medication like a paracetamol tablet that leaves a bitter taste in my mouth, or drink endless pints of water to get it to go down my throat. I've even got to the stage that if I needed to get medicine from the chemist I always ask for the liquid form, and you may laugh further here but that yellow amoxicillin antibiotic you get from the doctors is the exact same thing I would get instead of capsules or tablets that I just can't swallow.

Another reason to why I may have declined the medication was that in the position I was in at the time was a decent place, I was speaking to someone who I called my therapist, your mum was no longer in my house, she was no longer in my face, work was easing up as well as it could, I thought I could do it myself without any help. The doctors warned me that I needed to stay stress free, I had told them vague details of what I had been through, they told me it's the stress levels that cause my blood pressure to increase, and it's the blood flow which effects my kidneys inflaming. I thought I was strong; I was told without medication I had to drink plenty of water, eat plenty of fruit and vegetables and these were a must, and a balanced and regular diet was essential as well as regular exercise. I thought to myself and believed at that time I could do it, the only reason why I couldn't and wouldn't was your mum, but she had eased up on the stress she caused me and I really thought I was strong enough that even if she did start on me that I could and wouldn't let her get to me, what a big mistake that was.

ONE DAY IS ALL I ASKED FOR

There was a situation your nene was in Cyprus, I had taken two weeks off from work to look after you so that your nene could take this time off to do some bits she had to do. Unlike your mum who takes time off work to go away on holidays with many guys, it seems to be a different guy she goes with or a different guy she goes to see in Egypt. All I'll say there is, where's the priority? Your dad takes time off work to make sure you're looked after, and to give your nene a break as well, as well as the joy I get as I love to spend time with you, your mum, goes away to other countries to enjoy her life, to enjoy the life of not having the worry of a child, or commitments, this is why she can and will not worry about leaving you behind.

Then again why should she worry? She knows you're in good hands, the only hands and she knows it. In a normal day it's always me that looks after you, it's always me that has responsibility for you, I know if I'd go away, I'd struggle being away from you, what's worse I know you would struggle being apart from me, but I also know your mum would struggle looking after you on her own. I would worry if you were safe, if you were eating enough or drinking enough fluids, the worrying never ends with me, but that's what being a good parent is right?

YOUR MUM WOULD STRUGGLE WITHOUT ME

On this occasion where your nene went away, she couldn't get back as scheduled, I had an issue, I had to go back to work, I had already taken two weeks off to look after you, I asked your mum to look after you for just one day in the week until your nene came back, I've never asked for help from her ever before in regards to your care, all the other days I had covered with me, or family members such as your uncle, auntie and my teyze. Your mum refused, she said she didn't care, it wasn't her problem that no one could look after you and it was my responsibility because your nene had to stay away. At one stage she told me this whilst she was holding you in the rain without you wearing a jacket or a hood, she told me to organise who was going to look after you, all because I recommended your nanny to help out on the day I couldn't get covered as your nanny at that time was off from work.

What your mum did really upset me, got my blood boiling, she refused to take you out the rain, how do you think I reacted? I began to stress again, shout in the streets telling her to put you in the car or bring you back in the house, she said she didn't care, it's only a bit of rain, and, if you get ill, it's all my fault because your nene was away on holiday. My blood boiled, this is my daughter's mum not wanting responsibility, not wanting you, your mum is so happy being a part time mum, her life is more important than yours. As I got wiser, I realised why she didn't take time off work, she wanted to save her time off to go and meet her boyfriend in Egypt, so why should she waste her holiday or time off from work allowance on you, her boyfriend was always the winner.

SPENDING TIME WITH YOU IS BETTER THAN ANY HOLIDAY WITHOUT YOU

So who's this guy in Egypt? I don't know and to be honest I don't care. Obviously it all started when your mum went on holiday with my so called "work mate". According to your mum, apparently his true colours shone on this holiday and that he had abused her. Now whether I believe this or not this is what I was told from your mum when she got back from holiday. Was this true? At the time I thought it was, but as time went on I began to realise it wasn't, I should have realised from the moment your mum spoke that it was all going to be lies. Apparently he was a nutter; apparently he hit her, pushed her on to a table and then threw the table on top of her. Your mum on her return came to me asking me to get him beaten up. At first I actually thought about it, not for your mum's sake, but instead for yours, he ruined your life, but deep down I refused, I didn't want to bring myself to her low standards, I wanted to forget the past not relive it and bring it into my future.

As time went by, and for whatever reasons your nanny chucked your mum out of her house, your nanny has always said that she supported me, always said that she never agreed with what your mum was doing or had done; But these sort of comments would just make me think, I would put myself in your nanny's shoes, if you had been doing what your mum had been doing, believe me I'd be straight over to you and telling you what I thought. It got me thinking again, couldn't your mum see what she was doing was wrong? Because to me being a good parent means you should set an example, your mum wasn't doing that, instead she was doing things that would make my blood boil if I ever saw or heard you ever doing them in the future.

It had actually been quite peaceful since your mum had come back from holiday and split up with my so called mate. That is until one day, or one evening whilst I was away in Birmingham with work on our annual Christmas conference. I got a text from your mum, saying she had to move back into the house. My reply was "NO" your mum kept saying she had to, your nanny was going to throw her out, reasons I wasn't told, I was told she had to come because she had nowhere to go, in fact she even said she had to because there was nowhere for you to go. My response was easy, my daughter had somewhere to go; my daughter's mum had nowhere to go. This is when she said it was still her house.

Your mum always has another meaning to what she says

Her house was it? In the sixteen months and counting of us moving in, all she contributed was one thousand two hundred pounds, I on the other hand, paid every bill, which included the mortgage, council tax, gas, electricity, water, insurances, etc... bear in mind every bit of furniture and equipment in the house had all been paid by me as well, also note that I also paid all the deposit for the house, and all solicitor fees for us to move in, but apparently your mum being away from the house for ten months meant she was still entitled to come back as it was her house.

I should never have agreed to her return to the house, but I had you to think of, but also she said something that made me think.

You're all I care about, this is why I've written this book, so you know how much you are loved, and how far someone will go to show you.

Your mum knew that and still does and will always know I'd do anything for you, so she began to play games with my mind again, and this time she took it too far.

This is at a stage of my life, or shall I say a stage in the relationship where I was getting better mentally with the thought of what had happened, also the medical condition of my kidneys and blood pressure were not serious and could be controlled by me. I was content with everything happening, my therapy sessions dropped from once a fortnight to once every three weeks, if there is such a thing such as a good place, or a white light at the end of the tunnel, I was working my way towards it.

LIES, LIES, LIES

Your mum came round, told me how she realised what a bad mistake she had made, that the single life was not all it was cut out to be, she had acknowledged that no one would look after her better than me, seen and understood how such a good dad I was towards you, and apparently saddened of the thought we would never do family things again, as silly as this may sound she missed going out even if it was just to go shopping, maybe it's because she knew it was always me that brought the things when we went out. But most important reason she gave to me was that your mum said how it would be good for you to have both of us around so you can have a normal life. She wanted for us to try again.

What was I going to do? About two weeks prior to this, I was introduced through a friend to a wonderful girl, she was French and had a little girl herself around your age, she had come out of a relationship about a year prior to us being set up, she was in a relationship where she had been abused, she felt vulnerable. I seem to be a sucker for girls that aren't happy for some reason; it makes me feel alive and worthwhile by cheering them up. I had real high hopes for this girl and me, but your mum got in the way. After telling me all this, I agreed to give it one more shot with your mum. The next day I went round this French girl's house, because I couldn't just tell her by a text or by a phone call, I told her to her face that I wanted my family back. She was in tears, I felt sick, felt like a player even though nothing had happened between us, I felt horrible, like I used her emotionally, but you were my only thought, and all I wanted was for you to be happy.

I knew deep down I would never trust your mum again, not with everything I knew about her. I also knew this French girl made me smile, respected me, and actually looked after me more in two weeks then your mum ever did in our whole time together, but more importantly she felt my pain, she understood who I was and why I am the person I am today.

After I left that day I never spoke to her again, all I remember is her telling me to get out of her home, and her slamming the door as I walked out. I understand that reaction, and I even understand the reaction from my friend who had set us up, she told me to get lost and to never speak to her ever again, her actual words were, maybe you deserve to be unhappy, maybe just maybe you deserve everything you are going through, to date she is another friend I lost because of your mum, but what my friend had said made me think, was I making another bad decision?

I TRIED TO SAVE THE FAMILY FOR YOU

Your mum moved back in, and I had to cut ends with possible and potential relationships I could have had. I was talking to an old Turkish friend of mine, again in the same boat, had a three year old little boy, he was at the same age as you, she had been cheated by her ex, she wanted to go out on dates, but it never happened, mainly because I chose the French girl ahead of her and I didn't want to play games with people so I never took things to far until I was certain. I told her I just wanted to be friends and she agreed, however when I told her the circumstance I was in with your mum moving back, she told me what an idiot I was, she told me she didn't want to talk to me ever again, she must have thought I didn't want to be with her because of your mum and me wanting your mum over her. I know what she did was a bit harsh, but it's reality to where I am in my life, no one can understand or accept my life, and this is why I have put a hold on to my life until I can get your mum out of my life once and for all. Once that has happened, then and only then will I be content in looking for and finding someone worthy.

NO ONE CAN ACCEPT OR UNDERSTAND MY LIFE

Then there's the internet girl, who my mates think I met outside a fish and chip shop. I actually met this girl on an online dating website as sad and depressing as that may sound. I'm not going to lie, this girl and I are on the same wavelength, and we seemed to click mentally and are always on the same page as we spoke. The only issue I have with her is the distance she lives from me as she lives in South London, as well as the importance that I can't seem to find that spark inside me to want more than just being friends. What was I supposed to do? I had lost the French girl and also the Turkish girl as a friend, I was losing everyone because of your mum moving back in. I refused to tell her the truth because I just felt that it was best she didn't know, but more because maybe if I'm honest and say I felt deep down I knew that something would never happen between us but more because I needed an outside friend who didn't know what was going on, our innocent flirtatious chats helped me recover in the past, it made me feel important, made me feel wanted, is it fair to want to feel like this? I'm only human after all, not that people see me as one.

I know this girl wanted more out of us, but I couldn't, the travel would have been too much, but with your mums return I knew nothing could, or would ever happen, because if the roles were reversed I could never accept her circumstances.

So your mum moved back in, I cut contact with all my potential relationships, but the one sort of relationship I wanted in my life the relationship that I craved and deserved, the relationship I was so close to having was now far away. I made the French girl cry, but it was all for you, to be able to see you and hold you and know you are safe is all I want in life and to do that every day is my biggest dream, and my only dream I will ever have no matter how old you are.

YET AGAIN YOUR MUM THREW ME IN TO THE GUTTER

I even cut ends with my therapist; I had two reasons behind my thinking and actions. Firstly with your mum back in my life, there was no way I'd be able to afford forty pounds per session, because of your mum's money obsessed needs, even with your mum being in the house for just one day she was telling me to buy her an ipad for Christmas. Believe me I never had any intention of buying her any expensive gift, but I could see she didn't change, she was still after the money demanding, ego boosting things to make her the self centred, selfish person she is. Secondly, as much as my therapist had helped me, she disagreed with my decision to get back with your mum, on the last session I ever had with her, she told me I was a fool, told me I was going to be taken for a ride and that your mum was using my caring side towards you again to get what she wanted. My therapist was quite harsh, she told me to stop thinking of you, and to think of me. She was adamant with everything we had spoke about in the past that your mum was up to no good, and all the good work in trying to boost my confidence, my belief as well as my mind set was all a waste of time. When she said all this, I looked at her, I told her I wasted my money because I thought she knew who I was, I told her she should know that my daughter was my only thought in anything I did. I did say thanks to her, gave her the forty pounds for the session and walked out before my time with her had finished. I need to admit that she didn't want to take the forty pounds as we only spoke for less than thirty minutes, she tried to call me back, but I just continued to walk out the house, and didn't turn around to her calls to get me back.

Everything she warned me of, was right, I should have listened, If I wasn't so proud I'd love to start talking to her again because she helped me so much, I miss the chats I had with her, they were so useful, but yet again, your mum got in the way. Since your mum's return, I've held everything in within my head, I can't afford another therapist, your mum is making my house bills soar, so I only have one person who I am pinning all my hopes into, and that's me, so I've been sharing my own conversations and thoughts within myself, crazy I know, but I really have no other option.

Yes I know I need help, but I am proud, I don't know of the word defeat, you are my gold medal, and a lesson in life that I learnt from a young age was that you don't compete in something you can't win. Second place is still a race lost, and for me to admit I need help would mean I've messed things up so much that my gold medal may be lost and I will never win, I want to see my gold medal every day. Since you were born, you have been what I have lived and trained for, gone to work for you, battled the war for you, without you, what's the point? I really hope you understand what I am trying to say here, not just here; throughout this book I hope you understand everything. I don't think I am crazy, I just feel weak and tired of doing things alone and no one understanding anything.

MY THERAPIST WAS RIGHT

You, my baby girl, since your mum came back have been my saviour on many counts. Without your love and without the games and chats we have, I would have gone crazy, so thank you.

Your mum was still as secretive as anything and it was winding me up. We would go out for meals, cinema, guess who would pay? You got it, me. Your mum is so tight with money it's unreal, but with your mum it's the image scene that she has on her mindset. She needs to be seen as the centre of attention, she wants everyone to say positive things about her, and it's all games with her. Even when we did go out, and even on her return she would get her youngest brother, your uncle to listen out for you whilst you slept, you could call it babysitting, she would agree to give him money to do this, but on the way home your mum would always say she didn't have any money and for me to pay him. So it was more expense my way, but this whole babysitting arrangement with family's winds me up, when my family do it, they never ask for any money, even when friends of my family look after you, they never ask for any. In my culture even if we offered money it would be a disgraceful thing to even ask, but your mums side, away from your nanny, anyone who has to look after you needs to be paid. It seems to me like you're a burden to them, when in fact to my family you're a pleasure, I'm not saying that's true, although I would find it hard if it wasn't, I just hate the thought of having to leave you with someone who doesn't want to do it for the pleasure of being with you, especially if it's family involved. But then is it a wonder why your mum is so money orientated, if her own family want paying when looking after you?

IS THERE ANYTHING POSITIVE IN THIS STORY TO SAY ABOUT YOUR MUM?

I've always been the one who always takes you to the doctor, I'm the one who has never missed one of your injections, however there was an appointment for you to stay overnight at the hospital so they could see your sleeping pattern as you seem to struggle for air sometimes when sleeping, nothing serious, it's due to your tonsils and adenoid. She didn't want me to stay overnight at the hospital with you, it had to be your mum and she was adamant about it. It makes me laugh because she only wants it done or only wants to act like a mum so people can see her doing things for you, and the trend seems to follow course, because when we had your two year check up in the early stages of our breakup, she again came to this, but all she did was slag me off to the carer whilst I played with you, when I went back to talk to the lady I was told I had to help your mum set a routine for you. I was seen to be the disruptive one, I felt like saying to the carer, who is my daughter calling to the play mat to play with? Why do you think that is? Sometimes I have to bite my tongue, it's a good job I do think before I say or do something I may regret, because if I did say something, I know your mum would have said something along the lines of, "see what I mean, he is so difficult" and these are the sort of thinking's that wind me up, why are mothers needs considered more than fathers, we should be treated with the same respect, there are some fathers that do amazing things for their children and there is many mothers out there that play on this.

At the hospital that evening you stayed with your mum, I did try to leave whilst you were still awake, maybe to prove a point, but you wouldn't let me go. Instead you had to hold my hand to fall asleep on the bed, whilst all your mum did was complain she struggled to get signal on her phone.

As I was saying, I was suspicious of your mum on her return to our relationship; I approached her about it by telling her I didn't trust her and for her to make me trust her. In my thoughts there was no way I was going to be made to look like a fool again. She blatantly told me I was being paranoid, told me to just trust her, told me she had realised what she would lose if she lost me. Trust is something I will never ever do again for your mum, especially when she told me she got her cousin who owns a locksmith company to come in to my house and to break in to my filing cabinet and steal your passport and birth certificates whilst I was at work, is that not regarded as theft?

YOUR PASSPORT WAS STOLEN BY YOUR OWN MUM

Your mum kept telling me she was going to the sun bed near enough every day, over one hour later she came back from this apparent sun bed, however the longer she took, the more suspicious I became. I remember the days when we first got together, she used to go to the sun bed often, it actually only took her twenty minutes max to go and come back, but one evening my suspensions grew stronger. Your mum openly told me that she went to Egypt for just one day whilst we had been apart. I had to question her on why she went for just a single day? She told me she made friends out there. I'm sorry but that's crap no one goes out to see mates for just a day, especially your mum. From what I recall she has never done things on her own before, she would never even take you out alone even when you were a baby, she would always wait for me to come back from a long shift at work just to take you both out or I would have had an ear full from her as she would moan that she had been cooped up in the house all day and I didn't care about you or her. She wouldn't go shops, to the park, even doctors with you alone; she just never did anything alone. There was even this one occasion which I think is appropriate at this point of the story.

It was just when your mum first got pregnant, we were due to go on holiday and I was saving some holiday money in my draw, your mum knew I was doing this. Bear in mind, at this particular time your mum had not moved in to my home yet, her job at that time was near her mum and dad's place. The night before I asked if I should take her home as I had work early that morning, she said no it would be ok, as she didn't start till three in the afternoon and would use public transport to get there. This is how much your mum doesn't do things alone; she stole my money without asking me, all in aid to pay for a cab which came to near forty pounds. I only found out the money was missing because that weekend I went to put more money aside and realised I had money missing. I thought I was going mad, as on occasions I thought I was miscounting this money because some would go missing, little did I expect your mum to take it without asking. I have no idea how much your mum stole or took from me, but believe me I got your mum to pay the forty quid I knew about back in full after we got back from holiday and told her never to do it again, but when you think about it with more thought, maybe just maybe she's probably trying to steal my mum and dad's money now.

Anyways, back to the point I was making, I asked who this guy in Egypt was, and she told me there wasn't another guy. She also told me that she was planning on going to Egypt again in a few weeks, and that her going away shouldn't bother me.

MY GUT FEELING IS NEVER WRONG

My suspicions grew, I had to find out the truth and I mean I had to; I couldn't live the way I was, I was always questioning everything she was doing, I needed to know what was going on. The only way I would get answers to anything was through her phone, but your mum never left it alone, the phone was forever on silent which contributed to my suspensions that she was up to no good. That to me signifies that she didn't want me to know how frequent her phone was going off and in particular didn't want me to know who was messaging or phoning her, your mum wasn't stupid, she knew I'd question her if her phone was always going off. Didn't your mum learn from her last experience with me? Or did she think she was being clever and didn't think I'd put her in the same position as before? Did she think I'd be happy to be a bit on the side as she got to grips with another guy? But that was not all; your mum's phone was not just silent but was also always locked with a password. I agree in this day and age that all phones should have passwords because we store so much information on them that we are open to fraud. But luckily I got an evil eye, a clever eye you may say, especially when I am eager to get to know some truths so I watched your mum one evening unlock her phone as we sat on the sofa, I was pretending I was on my phone playing a game, but out the corner of my eye I saw and memorised her password as she logged in to her phone. I also knew her phone was left unattended under her pillow when she went to have her bath in the mornings, that was to be my cue to get the answers that would put my mind at ease.

I NEEDED TO CLEAR MY MIND WITH ANSWERS TO MY QUESTIONS

One morning I unlocked her phone, and there were messages I saw with my own eyes to a guy in Egypt on days that I was supposedly back in a relationship with your mum. I felt sick because I put an end to relationships that could have been and could have meant something to me especially with the French girl that I could have trusted in time especially in terms of trusting her not to hurt either of us. Instead I saw your mum texting another guy telling him that he was the only guy she would ever love, that she has never loved another man like she has for him and couldn't wait to see him. I wanted to scream the house down, I wanted to actually hurt your mum there and then, who would have blamed me if I went into the bathroom and held her head in the bath water until she drowned, but what good would have come from that, it's not my style, it's not who I am, and I respect myself, but I still respected her as a mum to you and there is no way I could hurt her. I breathed, and I understood what my family said to me. Don't touch her, she isn't worth it, you'll lose everything, the house, my job, my life but most importantly my baby girl. There was no way I was going to be made to look like a fool again, no way.

I found it difficult to accept that I had been played once before by your mum, I actually make myself feel sick that I never knew about it, but to think I was being played twice made me angry, all I could think about was what must she think of me, did she have no respect for me? Or am I right in saying that all your mum ever thinks about is herself and no one else? That night whilst lying in bed with her, I wanted to talk; she said she was tired, so she lay down to sleep. I, on the other hand had no sleep in me; all I had was anger and frustration so I put on my laptop to do some work. Your mum started moaning, telling me that if I was going to be on the laptop to go in the other room, I said no, in my head I was thinking that this was my room and I won't be driven out my own room. Instead your mum that evening got out of bed and went into the other room, what she didn't know was that I was extremely suspicious of her so I watched what she did in the other room through the crack of the door.

She had no intentions of going sleep, she wasn't going to sleep, instead she was messaging someone on her phone, she eventually came back into bed with me, and she was none the wiser that I had caught her out.

IT MADE ME FEEL GOOD

I again asked to talk, she refused sating she was tired, I just got out of bed and told her I was going out, I told her to stop me from going out. I had this contact on my phone that was willing and continuously asking me to go round her house for over six months, I'd resisted in the past as she means nothing to me, I knew that no relationship would ever blossom between us, but I was frustrated and annoyed of being made to look like a fool over and over again by your mum.

Your mum obviously didn't know about this girl, she even said, are you going out to cheat as I was getting dressed and putting aftershave on, I responded you'll never know if you don't talk to me, or you don't stop me from leaving. She allowed me to leave the house without asking where I was going; she was probably more interested in being alone so she could speak to this Egyptian guy. Whilst in the car I text her saying something on the lines of you have thirty minutes to call me or text me back, as well as saying that I couldn't believe that she allowed me to leave the house, I told her that her actions were showing that she hadn't changed, everything was still always about her. It's no surprise that I never got a response, instead I went and met this girl for an hour and went back home.

Am I happy with what I did? No, I'm not, but you get to a point in your life where you just give up, and that my dear girl was the moment I gave up with your mum, once and for all. I felt sick driving back home, I felt dirty, I felt confused, but ultimately I felt alone, felt I had no one to help me from yet another mistake I made by allowing your mum back. With the girl I just met, who wanted me to stay the night, someone that I don't show any attention or feelings towards was someone that wanted me, as strange as this may sound your mum made me feel like I was wasting away, but this worthless girl made me feel like I was worth something to someone away from you. Driving home from her house made me have a little smile, I felt I had something over your mum, I felt like two could play this game, your mum was playing a game with me, so I was going to play one with her, but I didn't want to play this game, I wasn't sixteen, I was a dad, this isn't what a dad should be doing, but this is what your mum was doing to me, and sometimes you react in the same way as how others treat you just to make ourselves feel better.

As horrible as this may sound, that night as I got back into bed next to your mum, in a strange but silly way, I felt good about myself, felt like I was more important than your mum, felt like I was better than her, although your mum didn't realise what I had done, to me it felt as if I taught your mum a lesson not to mess around with me. But that was it, after doing what I did I knew I would never ever want to be with your mum ever again, that much I realised, and that's why I did what I did so I could set my mind straight once and for all.

EGYPT OR YOUR FAMILY?

The day eventually came that your mum was going to Egypt, I can't even believe she wanted me to drive her to the airport, she was also adamant she was going to Egypt with work mates. I asked who? She refused to give me names, which again shows it's all lies that come out her mouth. There was no way I was going to drive her to the airport, instead I confronted her in the morning of her going, told her what I had seen on her phone, rather than own up to what she had done, your mum as always does she chose the path to lie, and this lie was the worst of them all, she told me that I had dreamt of seeing her phone messages, and that there was no way she was seeing anyone in Egypt. I wanted to take your mums phone and smash it, I told her to sign in to her phone and show me messages, and she refused telling me it was private. A learning curb for anyone here, especially you, if anyone loves or cares for you, they will always put your mind at ease, they will not play games with you, instead all your mum was doing was trying to cover her wrong doing up again. I told her if she wanted her family, she stays and fights for her family, I knew she would never choose us, even if she did, I would have thrown it back in her face, I really didn't want anything from her anymore, maybe just my pride back.

She kept saying she paid money and there was no way she was not going on holiday, I told her money means nothing, in life you need to realise there are things worth more than money, and I believe your mum chose what was out in Egypt ahead of us, I honestly don't care about me, but more importantly she chose what was out there over you. I gave her the ultimatum, Egypt or her family, she without hesitation chose Egypt. If I was in the position, I wouldn't think twice, I would have torn those plane tickets there and then.

That evening on my return from work, your Nanny came round to the house; I will always question the reason to why she did. Apparently your mum borrowed a cardigan of hers and informed your nanny to come around and collect it, as you can probably guess we could never find the cardigan your nanny came round for, we searched every room, every cupboard, and every little place a cardigan could go, but to no prevail. I know deep inside of me there was more of a reason to why your nanny came around, a reason I don't know, and I doubt I will ever find out, but one thing is for sure, I doubt it was for the sincerity of you or even me.

Whilst she was round, we spoke about what I found out in regards to your mum; obviously I knew your nanny knew, I knew your mum would have told her that I knew the truth, and I know your nanny knew about this guy she was seeing in Egypt, even prior to your mum moving back into our house to start again with me. Do you think that's right? Do you think your nanny put your mum up to it? Or was it all part of a bigger plan the two had?

WHY DID YOUR NANNY COME ROUND?

When your nanny asked me what happened, I told her I saw these messages, your nanny's response stuck in my head, rather than say who was it? Or who is it? Or what's his name? She just said "which one?" Is it me, or does that sound like your mum had a few guys on the spin at the same time? Does it sound like your mum had changed? My answer would be no, and I am sure the correct answer would be no too. There was no change, no effort to changing; all she did was lie to gain more for herself and no one else. What was I expecting, your mum was the same person if not worse than the person I knew in the past, and she was at it again. Your nanny also told me to throw her things away, and also told me that I should have broken your mum's phone, as well as her laptop, she couldn't understand how I was keeping my cool with her. Just so you know, something happened to a member of my own family a few years prior to this, where they were handcuffed and placed into a police car because they themselves with reason had broke and smashed someone's phone, I knew I had to keep my cool.

I was angry with myself, why did I let your mum worm herself back into the house? My life was getting better, but it was all for you, I just wanted you to have the life you deserve, and you need to believe I tried, and tried good and hard but I couldn't and will never be able to get over what your mum has done, she really has gone past the mark of no return.

Now your mum had moved in, she refused to go anywhere; she kept saying it's her home as well. Your mum lives in this fantasy world and will never grow up. If it was me that had made these mistakes, I would have owned up to my responsibilities and taken action, I would have left, because if I was your mum I would have nothing in the house that is mine, and I mean nothing, everything is what I've brought in and paid for, and I would have also realised my daughter is better off with her dad, would have left her with him, but made regular contact.

As I've said, your mum is selfish, has to do what she does and what's best for her and no one else. She knows I will never ever stop her from seeing and being with you. I want you to have a near perfect childhood, however that may never happen now, but you need to have both parents around to have that chance, but your dad has now put his foot down, and I am sorry you will never have that.

I HOPE YOU'LL UNDERSTAND MY DECISION ONE DAY

On your mums return from Egypt I packed all her things into black bags, I wanted her out, she said she didn't see him out there, as if I cared if she did or not, she tried to assure me he meant nothing, she said she was just after attention again. In my mind I was thinking here we go AGAIN, I didn't believe her, I really didn't. Why didn't I? Because why go looking for attention when you're trying to make your family work, she must have known this would be the last chance, surly she would understand that I'm only human, she must have realised I had trust issues, and I would watch every move and comment she made, but for someone that wanted to look for attention it was right from the start of us trying again. It hurt more because I probably lost someone in the French girl who really was someone who I could have seen a future with, if she ever reads this story, I'm really sorry for bringing more tears to your eyes, I really do hope you find someone who will look after you and care for you and your daughter the way you deserve. I hope you understand, but my little girl's future meant and still does mean more to me than anything, and I was gullible in trying to make it right for her.

Maybe if I never took the opportunity to try and save your family I'd never have been able to look in the mirror or give you a cuddle in the same way again. So maybe that's why I took a chance with your mum again, at least I know I did everything, at least I know in the future I will have a clear conscious and I will be able to eventually move on with my life when the opportunity arises.

Let me just clarify something I just said, yes I just said your future means more than anything to me, that doesn't mean I'll ever take your mum back now, that will never ever happen. Instead I'm writing this book, a book you will cherish, a story that will hopefully make sense one day, because I will always be there for you, regardless of where your mum is. I will always be there for your needs, which is why when your mum pulls you out of my arms, or takes you away as we play, it's all because in my eyes she is jealous of our bond and needs to get your attention away from me as it probably drives her crazy inside seeing you want your dad so much more then you need your mum. As she does this, you cry, to see you cry and see you pull your arms out wanting me to get you as you call for me, makes me go numb, deep within me it kills me at every instance and the more it happens, the more it drains me.

These calls and cries aren't something that developed overnight towards me, they have always been there for me, and I've only ever heard you cry for me and no one else. An instance that although is in the past now as you don't do this anymore, is when you used to cry every day, every morning when I used to drop you off to your nene so she could look after you whilst your mum and me went to work. These cries and calls really brought me down, made my day unbearable, to see your own child cry for you as you drive off, the look I saw in your eyes was unbearable, tears rolling down your cheeks, it made me feel like I was letting you down, like I didn't care. I can't explain how hard these moments were for me, I can't explain just how unbearable and weak these moments made me, but I hate seeing you cry, I hate seeing you in pain, and I hate being the reason for those tears.

I HATE SEEING YOU CRY FOR ME

Now your mum will probably say I'm just obsessed with you, but I call it being a father, I call it being a parent; your pain is my downfall. Eventually you eased off with the cries when I left you with nene, I believe this is because you realised maybe you could be a kid with nene and that you are just as safe with her as you are with me. Maybe the cries with your mum still exist because you can't be you, you can't be a child, you can't do what you want to do, and ultimately maybe you don't feel safe. I know you have to see your mum, I know you have to spend time with her, and I actually encourage it more then I'm given credit for, however when the most precious thing in my life is crying for me, and I can't do anything because I know deep down it will start an argument with your mum, I really have to refrain from doing this, so I have to let it go and cry within without showing no emotion. Just remember in this instance, although it kills me greatly, yes I do turn my back on you, but believe me I'm not doing it because I want to, but because I don't want you to see me crying, I don't want you to see me being weak, I don't ever want you to see me broken and hurt. Our bond I know kills your mum inside, but she has had opportunity after opportunity to put it right. I keep saying this, and I will continue to say this, why should I stop being the best dad I can, so I can make an average if that mum look good or better? I believe this statement is true, because the more I am not there for you, the more your mum will get your attention because you will begin to think my dad doesn't want me because I'm calling for him and he isn't coming to get me. So why should I make myself look bad? just so your mum looks good, the truth of the fact is, your mum should raise her game, your mum should start doing what I do, your mum instead of finishing work at four thirty every afternoon if not earlier, and going straight home to talk or Skype with her Egyptian boyfriend should want to go and pick you up and spend time with you, rather than wait for me to finish work, pick you up and take you home.

When we get home she spends as little time as possible with you before you go to bed. Now can you see why I call her a part time mum? You are not her priority, money and guys are all she thinks about when she isn't thinking about herself. I could never leave you alone whilst I went to another country to get it on with a girl, I'd constantly cry thinking and worrying how you are, for crying out loud I get upset when I have to work late and I can't see you before you go bed, I rush home hoping you haven't fallen asleep, when I realise you have, it drains my evening. Not being able to say goodnight and give you that good night kiss, which to me is so important is something that means so much to me that we have developed or shall I say adopted a good night song from the Disney channel.

WE HAVE OUR VERY OWN GOOD NIGHT ROUTINE

In saying that, I encourage you to say good night to your mum when I put you to bed, but recently I've noticed that your mum when she puts you to bed never sends you to me to kiss me good night, I wonder why?

maybe because it's a struggle for her to keep you away from me, a struggle to hear you keep telling her that you want daddy.

As you will know as you get older I lost my dad at a young age, I see many kids losing parents out of the blue, and depressingly I hear stories of children dying too. You never know when the last kiss good night will be, a lot of people say I'm negative, I call it best being safe than sorry. I'm always careful, always think things through; always wanting to make sure you are safe. Your mum keeps calling me a paedophile and obsessive, how on earth is that appropriate? Is it because I don't allow you to climb the stairs on your own? Is it because I play with you all the time? Or because I want to make sure you are safe and don't let you do dangerous things? Like allowing you to jump off the kitchen worktop into my hands, but most importantly I want to spend time with my daughter. I just want to see you grow, moments like this can never be replayed, once you miss out on these moments, they will be gone forever.

Doing this apparently in your mum's world, makes me a paedophile, and the accusation is worse as it is aimed towards me and my own daughter. I don't react to her comments anymore; I just get on with my life. Her jealousy towards me brings out her nasty side, a side in which will be her downfall one day, just mark my word on that.

BEING THE BEST DAD I CAN DOES NOT MAKE ME A PAEDOPHILE

Reacting to your mum as time goes on has got easier, because deep down I realise that my reaction is the reason that drives her on, but also its because I know what her and your nanny are up to. This may be untrue, but there are too many coincidences that show that I probably am not. You might remember I told you about my ex worker and your mum, well when I heard about them and realised everything, I acted like any normal guy would, I told your mum I would kill my ex worker. Why? Because I was upset, because I said if he ever hurt you then I would kill him in an instant, I also said if he tried to be a dad to you I would kill him too, it's all about respect, I would never let another woman mother you or hurt you, I'd expect the same back towards me, however your mum would do anything to hurt me, she would do anything to use you to get to me. So what did she do? She would record everything, all the conversations I had with her, she recorded me saying I would kill my ex worker! Why? Because maybe she had a game plan, maybe she wanted me to hurt him, so she could have a chance of getting my home, your home, money that doesn't belong to her. I only found out she recorded me, because the ex worker told someone I work with that told me to be careful. Majority of my staff respect me, they know how much I love you and how well I look after you, they would do anything for me, in particular looking out for me so I don't get into trouble. Although I never wanted them to know any of my personal business, it was nice I had their support.

When your mum split up with this ex worker of mine, and the accusations that she got assaulted on holiday were being branded, me being told to go beat him up because he split up my family, makes me think, what was she up to? I knew at the time she had this evidence on her phone. At the time she was seeing him she would phone me up telling me things just to work me up, to make me shout at her, and make me say I would hurt him. Your mum didn't care about how good a father I am to you, in fact all she cared about again was herself and how she could gain things for herself. I'm one hundred percent sure she would have gone to the police to turn me in if I did hurt him.

I WILL NEVER FORGIVE HIM

My ex worker did text me from Egypt on the day they were to return back to England. This text was my first acknowledgment that they had split. The text was simple; it was him trying to apologise to me, explaining that he had made a mistake, and that she was not worth the bother. He realised prior to them going away on holiday that your mum was selfish, self centred and uncaring, he realised her priorities were not where they should be and they should have been you which made her a bad mum. He told me that he'd done me a favour because he got her out my life. If thinking like that makes him feel better, then so be it, I will never ever forgive him, I may speak to him every now and then but that's only due to work related reasons. I will never ever shake his hand, maybe only when I get my life back on track and maybe when you understand a little bit, and you can give me a cuddle and tell me everything is ok, maybe then and only then I'll shake his hand, but till that day, my hand will never shake his.

That's not all, one evening when I got back from your uncle's house after watching football there, it was late, and as always you were with me. You had fallen asleep in the car on the way home, so I immediately put you to bed upstairs, when I came down, your mum just sat on the sofa with a smile on her face. I noticed a lighter on the floor; I asked whose it was? I was told it wasn't hers. During that week I'd found many lighters around the house, she didn't have a clue whose lighters they were or where they had come from. Unless you or me had started smoking she must have known, but she blamed your grandpa; as if I believed the story she was trying to tell me! I also noticed the latch for the back door was open, I asked why it was open, she said again she didn't know, whilst saying all this, all she did was laugh at me as if it was one big joke. I know that door was locked; I know I lock the doors before I leave. She was adamant she never opened it, as I opened the door and stepped outside, I smelt weed! I looked at her and asked if she had been smoking weed? All she did was tell me to stop being stupid and laughed at me. This was your home, my daughter's home, where I am trying to show you what is right and what is wrong, and your mother is showing you what is wrong all the time. I gave your mum endless opportunities to come clean and tell me the truth, but she was adamant she never opened the door. The lighters were not hers and the weed smell was not from her, whilst denying all this, all she did was smile and think I was one big joke.

That was it, I got the pillows off the sofa and started throwing them at her, telling her not to make me look like an idiot all the time, she just said I was crazy and went on the laptop, but your mum's laugh and childish ignorance annoyed me, so the last pillow I had in my hand I walked up to her and told her to tell me the truth, I placed the pillow with force on her face, I think your mum got scared, good if she did, she phoned your nanny telling her I was going to beat her up, I'm not stupid, I wouldn't touch your mum, losing everything I got for a little childish girl supposedly an adult, but more importantly why would I get in trouble and lose you? Your mum wouldn't know how to look after you properly so that would play on my mind. She kept annoying me, kept laughing so that's when I picked up her glass of water and splashed it in her face, I told her to snap out of what I would cast as being high. Your nanny phoned me up, threatening me that she would call the police, I told her I didn't care, I had done nothing wrong, your mum to me at that point was looking and sounding like a pot head, maybe this was a habit she had picked up from one of her boyfriends. She lied to me about the lighters; lied to me about the door being open, everything that comes out your mums mouth is lies, especially when I can tell the truth.

If the police had come, believe me they would have believed the non high person over the high person with no marks on her body apart from a wet face, which to my recollection is not a crime.

I TRULY BELIEVE YOUR MUM AND NANNY ARE UP TO SOMETHING

Your nanny's threat of calling the police on me rang alarm bells in my head. She knows her own daughter is in the wrong, and I understand ultimately where her loyalties will lie, but trying to get me into trouble for no reason is bang out of order, and you need to know this. How anyone can make an innocent person, a dad to their granddaughter, a father to their daughter as I am to your mum and they try to get me into trouble for their own gain is the lowest of the low, especially when I am the one who does everything for you and I do it the right way all the time.

It also got me thinking about what your nanny said to me the day she came round when your mum went to Egypt. Your nanny told me how she couldn't understand how I kept my cool with your mum; to me that sounds as if they are trying hard to break my patience, trying hard to get a reaction from me. I also remember your nanny telling me that "I should have broke her phone" "I should throw her things out" I believe this was in aid for them to think I had their trust so I could do some wrong doing towards your mum, and me thinking they were on my side, instead I would walk myself into trouble, because they would be on the phone straight away to the police.

It's lucky I have a cool head on my shoulders, and all I can say to them is that they should be ashamed with themselves because they aren't ever putting you first, it's always about them or your mum, no wonder your mum always thinks she is doing the right thing. As your mum ever been told by anyone out of her family that she is in the wrong? Or do they encourage what she is doing? I've lost total respect for all of your mum's family, because as I said it's bang out of order to get an innocent father into to trouble, especially when all he does is put an innocent little child which is you first at all costs. These games your mum plays all the time and some your nanny plays gradually, they are all games so I react and get myself in trouble, but as long as I have you in my thoughts, and know in my head that you would struggle without my care, keeps me away from doing the wrong that they want me to do. But just how much can one person take? I wonder how many people male or female have been tricked or played to doing something wrong for the gain of someone who does not deserve any gain.

I BELIEVE I AM BEING PICKED ON

Writing this has just made me remember an incident that occurred just after your mum had returned back to the house, again the more things that happen to me, the more I realise that maybe I am being picked on. Unfortunately not for the right thing which should be you, but I believe for the money your mum wants.

It was one evening and I was putting you to bed, and as all normal children do, you became cheeky from being over tired, trying to push my limits, but you knew the boundaries, however I raised my voice and said "Bed now or daddy will get upset" yes I raised my voice a little so you knew you were pushing the boundaries and for you to listen and calm down, but your mum came running up the stairs, ran straight up to you held your two arms and asked if I had hit you, your mum then said I don't trust you towards me, you're an animal and that she didn't know what I was capable of. I felt sick that she thought that, because I would never raise my arm at you, but the more I think, the more I believe your mum was high on drugs, because no matter what your mum thinks of me, she knows I'd never hurt you, maybe the drugs were getting to her or was the fact of her trying to get me in trouble the reason for her outburst? Either way, it's got me thinking.

Trying to teach you what is right and what is wrong is so hard, I show you love and attention and spend time with you to show you the true meaning of love, don't get me wrong, I do tell you off, and I do shout at you when you do something wrong, when I say shout I don't literally shout at you, I raise my voice but only when I know you know deep down that you know when you have done something wrong. I don't do it in such a way like your mum, who ignores you, and whilst you try to get her attention, she tells you to F*%k off, I realised that someone had been teaching you this word, or you had picked it up from somewhere. It was clearly from your mum, I questioned your mum about it, all your mum said was "oh it must be from your nanny because she always says it". When you first said the word to me, I questioned you after telling you off, I asked who said that to you, you said mummy, and I know you wouldn't lie to me.

THIS VIDEO COULD AND WOULD RUIN YOUR MUM

With this in mind, I have a video on my phone that I have saved on many media banks, just in case I delete or lose it from one. It's a video that makes me cringe, a video that shows me exactly everything your mum is. The video is of me and you, a video of me asking you questions like are you sleeping and you then pretend that you are, a video of where I ask you where your nose is, where your eye is as well as other parts of the body are, to which you show me by pointing to them. However you keep touching your mum's hair by accident because you can't keep still as you are sitting on top of the back of the sofa. Bear in mind your mum is on her phone, I think it's important I mention that but it's no surprise as that's all she does. Rather than moving away from you by just a little bit if you were bothering her that much, she takes it in her stride to shout at you and scare you which is obvious in the video as you jump, but she doesn't just shout at you, she swears at you and warns you! Warns you from what? Well, you accidentally do it again and this time she drags you off the sofa. Your mum at the time told me to delete the video, I told her I did, but I never, maybe this is the only chance I will have of her true colours being shown, but that's not the only thing I've recorded. I've recorded you crying and calling out for me, telling your mum you don't want her and that you want me, I have your mum telling me to go away because you have to get used to being with her. I question why you are the one that has to get used to her? You never had a choice when you were little, you only had me as an option, you're used to being safe with me, and you're used to my way of things now.

It's not your fault your mum chose to be ignorant towards you; it's not your fault your mum chose other guys ahead of you. You're not a toy, and your mum can't turn the on/off switch as and when she likes or is it better to say when it suits her best, having a child you should be there for them twenty-four seven not when it's convenient for themselves.

I'm sorry, the damage was done when your mum neglected you and still does as I write this book. She left me to do all the work, left me to bring you up at a time of your life where you were learning, at a time you were understanding who is there to care for you and who is not but most importantly who you can and can't trust. This is why you're a daddy's girl, and this is why she will never have the bond you have with me, but I shouldn't be punished for this, instead be rewarded for what I did, but like everything it's not about what I want, for me the most important thing is that you shouldn't be punished for something you haven't done wrong.

CREDIT SHOULD BE GIVEN TO THOSE WHO DESERVE IT

I stated a little while ago that I don't get the credit I deserve for trying to get you to want your mum, for trying to allow you to leave my sight with no fears. These tantrums of you wanting me, the fear I see in your tears and cries started when your mum moved out, from the moment you were staying overnight at your nanny's house with your mum on the occasional nights. At first on your mum's days she would drop you off to nene in the mornings and pick you up, I was being stubborn, I wanted to prove to her that her choice would bring complications to herself, would put her out and realise it's not easy to do all this work, and although she did ask me to take and pick you up, I continuously refused, but I did eventually give in to her requests. A lot of people will say WHY? But only if you're a parent in my position and have my thinking and feelings towards my child then and only then will you ever understand. I missed you so much, a night away from you is like the biggest torture I have ever experienced, and to think in the future that I may not see you for weeks drives me crazy. I used to plan for the future, but now I can't because the future can look a little blurry. I now only live for each day, I cherish every second I can be with you, I've learnt that you don't know what's around the corner, and I believe my actions that I do everyday are the actions which will help my future.

So I gave in to your mum's request, but I was being selfish, I wanted that half hour plus in the car taking you to nene, I wanted that half hour plus taking you back to your mum after picking you up, that was all for me, I wanted to know you were safe, I wanted you to know daddy had not gone away, I wanted you to know daddy still loves you more than he ever has, and I did this by just being there for you and showing you my love.

Those conversations we have had in the car are so precious to me, I've seen you grow up with the conversations we have had. Conversations that I value so much as it has given me sentimental memories, these conversations ended up in me switching the car radio off for good, because of what was coming out from you was more important than anything talk sport would ever say. From the first moment you seeing a dog and saying woof to me, which soon went to look daddy a doggy, then daddy look two doggies to now look daddy small white doggy or big spotty doggy. I've seen you grow and because the future looks unclear it makes me sad, but on the positive note you being a daddy's girl and wanting your daddy all the time is the only thing that makes my future look bright.

DADDY WILL ALWAYS COME BACK

So what credit do I deserve? When I used to pick you up, you used to ask me, or say, daddy house or nanny house? When I told you was going to stay with mummy at nanny house, you used to cry and actually have tears in your eyes, I used to tell you that mummy had to see you, had to spend time with you, just like daddy had to. No matter what I said you just didn't want to go, the journey to your mum was me convincing you that you had to stay and for me to promise you that daddy would come back. This is the moment where it all started, from here on in, every time I would leave your sight you would ask me if daddy was going to come back? Of course I always said yes. It's amazing that at such a young tender age you needed and wanted security of knowing that I would be coming back to look after you. Even your nene tells me, whenever your mum went to pick you up, you would cry because you just didn't want to go.

On the plus side, the days where you were staying with me, the days you asked if you were staying with me, and when I said yes, it's the biggest smile I ever saw, you were happy, that's the part of being a dad that makes it all worthwhile, that moment your child is happy, is happy because she wants you, because you're the one that makes her happy.

After your mum moved back in, when I used to pull up at the house, as soon as you saw her car on the drive way, you would say you didn't want her in the house, in your own words you would say "tell mummy go away" and even "I don't love mummy" although it boosts my daddy ego to hear that, as a father who wants the best for his daughter that's the worst thing I could hear.

YOUR MUM IS THE REASON YOU HAVE NO HOME

The fact your mum was back in the house and I deliberately don't want to call it a home, has made you not want to come back to the house, not want you to come back to what should be your home. You began to ask me when I picked you up if mummy was home, when I said yes, you would tell me you didn't want to go home, you would say you want to stay at uncle's or nene's house. Again it was down to me to talk to you, for you to understand that she's your mum, conversations that I didn't want to have but conversations I did have, and conversations that no one knew I was having, believe me I doubt after all your mum has done to us, any other man in my shoes would not have been this positive about your mum to you. I know in the future these unbiased conversations I have had with you, will probably come back and haunt me, but you know what, it was the right thing and the best thing for you and no one else, not even me, so it was the right thing to do.

I can't get it into my head why you're like this with your mum, yes I know you're really close with me, but she's your mum, however I truly believe you understand the neglect you have been given, you understand maybe the pain your mum has given your dad and maybe it's your way of letting her know that daddies the one. The biggest thing in my eyes that doesn't help your mum is that when she pulls you away from me, you see someone telling you that you can't be with the one you want to be with, instead of taking time to get your trust, getting to your level and doing the things you do, all you saw was someone taking you away from something you wanted, hence the reason why you feel that she is the reason to your bad times, the reason to not being able to do what you want.

The thing that gets me, you get punished and so do I, but the thing is, I'd be doing the things I do, I would be the person I am to you whether I wasn't with your mum or was. As people say the proof is in the pudding, and I know hand on heart I would still be doing what I do for you anywhere, anytime, and in any circumstance, it's just who I am.

CIRCUMSTANCES MAY CHANGE, BUT I WILL NEVER CHANGE HOW I AM WITH YOU

I've never played mind games with you, I've never once told you to hate your mum, never once told you that daddy is better than mummy, but in your mum's eyes she constantly accuses me of this, constantly telling me why I say certain things to you. She doesn't understand that you have your own mind, you pick up on conversations, you're at a learning age that you pick things up very quickly, and sometimes mimic what you have seen and possibly heard.

Now you're used to my house being my house, and one day you asked your mum "why was she living in daddy house"? Now I heard her quietly tell you its mummy's house as well, but you wouldn't have it, you kept telling her it was daddy's house. Your mum ended up confronting me asking why I was telling our daughter that the house was mine? Well the truth is that the house in my eyes is mine, but the false accusation is that I never once told you anything like this, as I said, you see and notice things all the time.

There was a moment you were looking at photos of you as a baby on my phone, and as you do, you asked questions, you asked one particular question whose house the photo was taken in, when I said that was daddy's old house, you began to say you didn't want to live in this house but live in daddy's old house and to be a baby again, you said this to your mum, and again your mum thought I was putting you up to saying these things, telling her that you want the old house.

If your mum, actually took time to talk to you, and listen to you, she would understand who you are, she would understand how you react and what you say and why you say it. An example was Christmas 2013 of your mum buying you a bike that was too small and a year to little for your current situation as you are taller than the average child in your age group. To me this is evidence enough that she really doesn't know you well enough, your mum should know everything about you, should know what you like, and what you don't, but ultimately who you are.

THERE'S ONLY ONE PERSON TO BLAME

All these flashbacks really wind me up, I constantly get accused by your mum, trying to blame me for things she doesn't like that is happening or happened. She is the sole person for her downfall in the relationship between you both, but as your mum does, she blames everyone but herself. You even told your mum to give me money one day, because I told you daddy had no money because he was paying all the bills, food, and that you had to wait a week before I could buy you a toy you wanted. Your mum thought you told her that she was taking my money, which in theory again is kind of true, but that's not what you said; all you said was something along the lines of give daddy money then again I've always learnt that sometimes we misinterpret things because we think the truth and can easily mistake words spoken to what we truly think of the situation.

MONEY, MONEY, MONEY

Just a quick mention about money, since your mum's return back to the house she hasn't paid or contributed to a single bill, no contribution to any gas, electricity or anything. In fact she begun to eat my food, drink all the tea, coffee, eat the chocolate that I brought for you, use all the sugar and then because there was no other sugar in the house she would just start using the caster sugar I used for baking cakes with you, she ate the cooking chocolate we melted for cakes, because she must have had a chocolate craving, but these are not one offs they happen all the time. My bills since the return of your mum to the house rocketed up by more than two thirds to what I was paying previously without her. Was and is this fair?

It got to the stage with money that I did nothing for me with any of the money I earned; every penny I earned was providing a roof for you, me and your unwanted mum who was spending my money without knowing it. I had money problems and this was most obvious when my car broke down, and needed over a grand to repair. I didn't have that money, and it was the hardest thing in the world for me to ask my mum to lend me money to pay for it. This is money I will one day pay her back, I am no charity, and I won't take handouts to ensure I get by. That moment of time it made clear sense of what your mum brought me down to, I used to be so independent, it was obvious I was now in a deep hole that your mum had thrown me into and I was now struggling to keep afloat of everything.

I WILL SOMEHOW, SOMEDAY PAY MY MUM BACK

Some of the things your mum does are so shocking, and it's no surprise to why my bills have soared so much. The heating never switches off, why should it? When your mum doesn't pay a penny towards it, funny thing is one evening I went down to switch it off before I went to bed and I found your mum in her bra and knickers in the living room on the sofa as she was on her laptop. God knows what she was up to, I really didn't want to know, but if you really do think about it clearly, you'll understand exactly what she was up to. Believe me this incident really began to stop me wanting to go into my own living room. She told me she was hot, as if I believed her, but if she was that hot, why didn't she just turn off the heating? If she's so cold, put on a jumper, but then again its inconsideration towards other people, that's who your mum is. I believe I've said and used the words before, selfish and self centred.

Some of the other factors to why my bills have gone up, hair dryer on every morning for around an hour, no wonder her hair dryers always break and she has to keep taking yours, what about using the tumble dryer? She doesn't use it like a normal person, your mum takes the clothes straight out the washing machine and puts them in the dryer, and at times one garment at a time, and the annoying thing is that she just leaves the dryer on for ages. What about cooking? Your mum doesn't cook normal or fresh foods from scratch, but she likes her Kiev's or frozen chicken breasts, it's a simple dish to make as all you do is place them in the oven. Normal people would remember that these are in the oven, however your mum forgets, and even on one occasion left the house with the oven on. Luckily I came back just in time, the kitchen was full of smoke, and inside the oven was what looked like two chicken breasts but burnt black. I quizzed your mum on this, I was told she only left the house five minutes before I got in, and was only going to be gone for ten minutes, is it a surprise that your mum didn't come back till two hours later? I hope your getting the jest of this now, forgetful, no consideration, no respect, no responsibilities and the biggest two words selfish and self centred.

YOUR MUM HAS A FREE LIFE

Your mum wasn't buying any washing powder, detergent, and to date still does not buy any washing up liquid, no toilet rolls, and she uses this like it grows in the garden, this is going to sound silly but I only brought twenty-four rolls in the ten months she was absent, I was now going through a minimum twenty-four a month. As for kitchen rolls I have no idea what she does with them, it just got out of hand. This might make you laugh but there's been times where I came home to find out the toilet paper had run out, and as your mum refuses to buy any, she used kitchen roll and blocked the toilet, as ashamed as she should have been, she showed no fault and left the toilet blocked, guess who had to unblock the toilet? Yes it was me.

To top it all off it got to the stage after Christmas where I had brought a box of Ferrior Roche as a present for a friend's birthday, now I had put it away till the day I needed it, when the day came for me to get it and give it to them, I noticed it had been opened and some had been eaten, when I asked why? Your mum's response was simple; well it had been sitting there for ages. Where's the respect? None for me it's obvious, but where was your mum's self respect? She has none, because it's all about her needs and no one else's. Your mum did pay for this in the end, but that's because I really put on a big fuss about it.

I'd even get a text from your mum saying she's eaten the pizza out the freezer that I got myself, and that I should replace it, what goes through your mums head, no one knows. It's got to the stage that I can't do a week's shop for groceries, I can't stock up, especially on tins of tuna, pasta, biscuits, chocolates, crisps, yogurts, fruit, vegetables, even ready meals. I've always been brought up to never argue or deny someone who was hungry or thirsty but this was out of hand now, I didn't mind your mum using my milk or bread, but getting requests to buy specific milk for her was a bit out of order I thought. You see I brought blue top as that's what you drank, but I was asked to get green milk next time I get milk because that's what your mum wanted, don't worry I always just got the blue.

GET ME GREEN MILK

It's ridiculous really, as I said it's lucky I was brought up with respect, and with the knowledge that if anyone needed food or drink you allow them to have some. But getting requests such as the milk made me laugh, I'd get texts from your mum asking me to get some tea bags, no ordinary tea bags but the expensive ones, again I didn't buy them, and in time I refused to buy tea bags full stop, I don't have a cup of tea, if I do it's like once a month, but all the tea bags I have disappear out the house within a week or two, again I just left it, I didn't question it, I just couldn't be bothered to start an argument. But as time went by I began to notice that a can of beans I brought myself went missing, the tuna cans, even Weetabix. I actually brought a pack of thirty-six Weetabix, you had two for breakfast one morning, the week after I go to give you breakfast, bear in mind you always have breakfast at nene's so they shouldn't have been eaten, as I opened the draw, I only have twelve left. I know where they go, and it answers the mysterious question to the missing beans, weetabix, tuna, tea bags and even more foods.

I got a feeling your mum takes them to work, as one morning I caught your mum placing tins of tuna in her handbag as she was going to work, I didn't say anything to her, maybe I should have, but my look should have been enough to tell her to stop, but she didn't and she hasn't, but then again what do I expect from a self centred and selfish individual who only thinks of themselves? As far as she knew, all the things she took that weren't hers may have been something I was planning to give you, so in theory you could have gone without because your mum took it, with this in mind you could say I've been paying for your mums breakfast, lunch, possibly dinner, and all her drinks at work, is that fair?

I told your hala about this, she thought it was funny, if I told others I'm sure they would ask why I let it happen. I let it happen because if I didn't,

I'd lose you, not in the sense that your mum would take you, because I wouldn't let that ever happen, but I'd lose the fact that I see you every day, and I'd rather go through the torture that I do, for that amazing feeling of being around you.

OUR BOND JUST GREW STRONGER

That was your mum's biggest mistake in my eyes, coming back into the house she wasn't welcome in. Firstly by me, and secondly by you, the mistake was that I was slowly getting used to not seeing you every day whilst you stayed with your mum, mentally I was getting better, but now I know I can't go through that again. The second mistake was that her coming back, grew our bond stronger, made you realise you did have a choice, a choice that maybe you didn't know you had. It made you realise daddy wasn't going anywhere, made you see who was the one who treated you better and made you realise you deep inside yourself wanted your dad more than your mum. Because with the two of us around you, you had that choice of who you wanted to be with, and it was always a proud daddy that was your choice, but even when this happened, your mum just sat there and let it happen, that again was a big mistake, she should have done what she could to get your attention, she should have played games with you, I would never have not allowed her, in fact I wish she did, because the more you clung on to me, the harder it is for either of us to let go in the future.

Your mum will always be in denial, she can't see outside her own head, outside her own world, what she thinks is happening is happening, when she sees you cry it's my fault, when your mum and me came to an end it was my fault, when I was tired it was my fault, when I want you and want to hold you it's my fault I can't, anything bad that's happened is my fault. Your mum will always say the relationship between you two was perfect, it's amazing how spending as little time with your daughter and not seeing her grow up and know what sort of a person she is becoming is acceptable, but the thing is, from my eyes, and anyone who could see in, knew the truth, they knew that your mum wasn't perfect, it really was far from that.

TROPHY MOMENT MUM

You must be thinking surly my mum spent time with me? Yes she did, however as I keep saying it only happens when it suits her or when it's a trophy moment. I'm not sure if such a word or statement as trophy moment exists but from what I have experienced I believe this is the only word to sum up your mum's actions. She only wants you when it suits her, never will she go out her way to pick you up or drop you off for the sake of being a mother, in fact when I've had to work early or late she puts up a big fuss about it, also recently as I write this part its July 2014, I'm regularly getting texts saying "can your mum (which is your nene) have her tonight?", some of the excuses I got is that your mum was working late. From experience your mum never works late, and being the sort of guy I am, I asked a mate of mine whose girlfriend lives in the area to drive past the house at half past five and tell me if there was a car parked on my drive way. The answer I got back was yes, there's a BMW parked there, this mate of mine does not even know your mum has moved herself back in to the house, nor does he know she got herself a new car. Explain to me why then she refused to pick you up? Believe me I would do anything to spend time with you, in fact your mum once said to me along with being obsessed with you, that I love you too much and that I need to stop being there for you all the time.

Am I wrong to think that there is no limit to how much you love your child? Now I can't expect you to ever understand that comment until you one day have kids, but many parents like me, or sane parents out there will understand that you cannot put a limit on the love you have for your child. As for having to stop being there for you all the time, the only reason I can think she wants me to do that is to make herself look better, for her to gain some sort of grip of being a mum. It just saddens me now days, even worse is that I'm used to it and I've given up hope in your mum actually being the mum I want her to be for you. "Trophy moments" will come for your mum, such as Christmas, birthdays, parties, Mother's Day, but these days will come and go, it's the other days to me that count, the days that are normal days, raining outside so we play some games, we paint, we draw, we hide and we seek, we cook, we dance, we sing, we clean, we shop, I take you everywhere I go, not because of what your mum thinks that I'm obsessed but because doing everyday things are what counts and that to me is what being a dad is all about.

I LOOK FORWARD TO MY DAYS OFF

I look forward to my days off from work because I know that's daddy and daughter time, your mum on the other hand, from what I see, and what you tell me, she seems to push you aside to your nanny so she can have her own time on her only day a week that she can spend a whole day with you alone.

As a father you're the only trophy I need, to me it was upsetting that this is how low your mum thought of me, I understood we broke up, but I still got your mum a card and little present from you on Mother's Day, may I add this though and this may be important, even though I buy these, especially the card, I'm wise with what I buy, as I don't want to send the wrong signal out. In particular the card, I ensure that there is no sign of or any message that reads anything such as "best mum" I get a card that simply reads happy Mother's Day, why should I lie to your mum? If she deserved it, then yes I would get it. It was shocking that on my first birthday after we broke up, I got nothing, not even a card from you, but still on your mum's birthday and Mother's Day I still got a card and a small present, I even got a request once as a text from your mum saying that if I was struggling with ideas of what to get her for Mother's Day then to get her a mug, I would be the mug if I brought her the mug as requested, no pun intended.

I REFUSE TO BUY CERTAIN CARDS

When your mum and myself were together, you would think it was a mutual relationship, believe me we were never mutual, the days where I asked your mum to drop you off or pick you up, she demanded I paid her petrol money, the love of your child should have been enough to do it, but again like everything I write, surely this is painting that picture of what I had to go through, and yes was the answer to your mums demand, I had to give her petrol money just to make sure my daughter was picked up and safe, as I said all your mum is interested in, is money.

On one occasion I had a single rose delivered to her work trying to be romantic with a question mark on the note, apparently she hit a car because she was stressed from who was sending it to her, maybe she was trying to figure out who sent it, maybe her boss, the fifty year old co-worker, maybe my co-worker, maybe her cousin's boyfriend, maybe me, or maybe someone else. Guess who had to bail her out with money to pay the other driver, just so it didn't go through insurance? You got it, me. Who paid for her tyre to be replaced because she got a flat tyre picking you up, and it was my fault she had to go that route? You got it right it was me, there are way too many occasions, but money is what drives your mum forward.

I first noticed your mum's obsession with money on one of her birthday's when we first got together. I've always hated people, grownups that demand things on Christmas and birthdays, to me being and knowing someone should be about them, not the gifts they can buy you, but on this occasion it wasn't what I brought her but what my mum, your nene gave her as a present. Now your nene is probably the worst person in the world at getting presents and just gives money, she gave your mum forty quid, her response towards my mum at that time was like she was the queen, all happy, all joys, and your mum even told me she couldn't believe my mum had given her forty quid. I got a feeling those sort of good will gestures that me and my family did towards your mum, as well as accepting her into the family with open arms is what opened her eyes to what we had and is what she truly wanted in the relationship with me. I can't put into words just how your mum reacted on seeing the money my mum gave her, she childishly was jumping up and down. Just like everything your mum did, I really didn't think much of it, I just thought she was happy that my family accepted her, but I didn't really take a minute to think that it was more to do with the money than any other aspect towards a gift that was given.

MORE PROOF THAT MONEY MAKES SOME PEOPLE SO HAPPY

Your mum never ever gave, she just kept on receiving and this is something that in time will ruin her, because no guy, no decent person will ever accept anyone like that to come into their life. As I always say, it's you I feel sorry for, because you are going to have to go for a ride on a roller-coaster with your mum, and I am so scared and worried of how you will be brought up in my absence.

There are days that your mum texts or calls me to tell me she wants to pick you up, the problem I have with this is that she does this last minute, and it winds me up because your nene may have planned to do something with you, which on one occasion was the truth and it upset your nene. When I question your mum why, she says she doesn't care and that she is your mum and that's final, your mum really does not care about anyone else but herself, we all have to answer to her needs there and then. I just let it happen because I want a simple life, I don't want you in a life where everyone shouts and moans, so I take all this stress inside me. Everything your mum does stays inside me though and it angers me, your nene and everyone moans to me that your mum's being out of order and for me to do this and to do that, it all adds up fuel to my stress levels because I just walk away from potential arguments, because these arguments just drain me, I just want you to be happy and that's it, it shouldn't be hard to achieve this.

On the occasions when I ask why she wants to pick you up, it's not because she wants to spend time with you, but more to do with the fact she wants to take you to her cousins house or she is going to her mum's which is your nanny's house, again another "trophy moment", as your mum shouts at everyone "look at me everyone, I'm a mum and I'm perfect in every way".

IT'S ONLY EVER DADDY YOU RUN AFTER

I even know the tactics that your mum uses to get your attention when it suits her, as I've said before when all three of us are in the same room, you always play with me, if I leave the room, you come running after me asking where I am going, on the other side if your mum left the room, you would be none the wiser and not be bothered. The example I am going to use is more to do with my pet hate I think then anything, but to me results are what counts, and when you come to me and say what didn't happen upsets me, as it's always false promises from your mum to you.

When I am going out, I tell you straight where I am going, going supermarket, and you know the name of all the big supermarkets, even the name of the supermarket I work for, you actually enjoy coming to my workplace as you think it's fun. If I'm going nene's, or uncle's or hala's I tell you that's where I am going, but when your mum wants you to go with her she won't just say I'm going nanny's or I'm going to the shop or wherever she'll be going, it's how she tells you it that annoys me. In a childish over exaggerated voice she promises you things that won't happen all the time, promises you that nanny has the swimming pool up in the garden, that she will take you to the park, buy you chocolates, on several occasions, more than most they are false promises. When I ask how your day was, and what you did, rather then you tell me what you did, you tell me what you didn't in a sad voice, sometimes you tell me that you didn't do anything, or you went nanny house and mummy went away, sometimes you tell me that you and mummy went to the shops, but mummy didn't buy you a toy. It's kind of just hit home as I write that last statement; away from chocolates I don't recall your mum outside your birthday and Christmas buying you any sort of toys.

NO CHILD SHOULD EVER BE GIVEN FALSE PROMISES

I do have to say one good thing that's been happening recently, you're mum, although I deep down think it's your nanny's idea as well as your nanny who actually takes you, is that you go swimming lessons every Saturday afternoon. Although I also need to state that if your mum doesn't want to have you on the Friday night as I have work extra early on a Saturday which means I am unable to look after you on Friday nights, and this would mean that I would be unable to take you nene on a Saturday because I wouldn't be comfortable waking you up so early. Or on occasions if your mum is to go out all day on the Saturday, you normally do miss these swimming lessons because you're staying with nene, or auntie or even hala on that Friday night. I think that's a brilliant idea though that you're having swimming lessons, and it at first was comforting to me that your mum was showing interest and wanting to be with you, but I realised as weeks went by when you would tell me mummy didn't take you and nanny took you, and when I ask where mummy was, you would reply mummy take me nanny and mummy left. Either way it's good that it's productive, I just wish your mum was doing it and not your nanny.

I really am not moaning, I think if your mum had been closer to you, then I believe I would have struggled a lot more, you were my rock, you were the reason I got up and fought, I got battered and bruised every day, but you were my reason and my only reason to carry on. Knowing your mum wasn't there for you, the thought that you would struggle without my input, dedication and love just made things so much easier for me, and as some people have said to me, what I've done and been through has made me became a mother and father figure to you all in one.

It actually is very flattering when people on Mother's Day send me messages saying, I know today is for mothers, but some mothers don't deserve the celebration, in my eyes you truly are the best mum and dad a child could ever wish for. That my dear girl, makes everything worthwhile for me, just to know the outside world can see exactly how I am doing and coping, because there's times with the line of work I do, the way I look after you, and the travel I do, nothing else comes into matter. I even ignore phone calls from my family and friends now days, because I just don't have the time or patience to deal with anything that really doesn't matter to me.

I CAN'T EXPLAIN JUST HOW TIRED I AM

Which brings me to where I am now, I'm weak and tired as I write this, there's nights I just have no strength and fall asleep so quickly, there's even times when I put you to sleep, I just fall asleep at the same time as you if not before. Your cries that call for me drain me, I wish I could just hold you and not let you cry, but then your mum would moan that I'm being a paedophile again, would moan that I'm not letting her be a mum. The truth is, I want out, I want to get away from your mum, your mum isn't going anywhere on her own will, and I'm even thinking of giving her money from the house just so I can move on with my life, but then what happens to you? your mum doesn't think these things, your mum uses people not things, and loves things and not people, whilst I'm visa versa. Since she came back to the house, I've never had one lay in, she has the luxury of being whatever she wants, all I ask is for one Sunday morning to sleep in, when I ask, the response I get is that you want your daddy, so I need to stop doing what I'm doing and look after you. There was a night in July 2014 when I went out on a Saturday evening, I got back about three in the morning and probably fell asleep about four, you woke up at six, came running into my room as you always do and jumped on top of me wanting to play, I asked your mum to get up and look after you, her response which upset me more was, I get up early on a Saturday to look after her when you go work, how annoyed do you think I felt, every day I look after you, I ask for one day and that's the response I got.

ALL I ASKED WAS TO HAVE ONE LAY IN

I shouted at your mum because I was tired, she eventually got the hump and went downstairs with you, but the anger and fume I had within me did not allow me to go back to sleep after that, especially when I could hear you talking to your mum asking where daddy was and that you wanted to go upstairs to daddy, but you know what? Even on the rare other occasions I went out, I remember an instance with my best mate when we went out, I got back at six in the morning, I think you got up twenty minutes later, your mum never flinched it was me again that looked after you. Apparently all this is my fault, I've allowed this bad habit your mum has to develop and happen, but believe me, anyone in my shoes would have no other option but to be like this. On saying this let me get this in to context though, since your mum came back, I've gone out twice, why? Because I'm ashamed to invite my mates round. My best mate is no longer a friend, he always asks to go out, but I can't admit to him your mum is back in this house, I can't bear to talk to him, I can't explain how stupid I've been, I can't invite him round, I can't do anything. I have to keep giving him the same excuse that I am tired or ill just to make him leave me alone.

I'm ashamed to ask my family to come round, I'm ashamed of everything your mum has done, but more to do with the fact that I know if I go out, I'll be more exhausted then I already am, it's not worth it, you're my priority and I'll save my energy for you, but it's fair to say, I do need a night out to let my hair down. Your mum does this on any occasion she wishes, she goes away on frequent holidays, nights out, without a think of who is going to look after you, why? Again it's all because your daddy is there to look after you and will do anything for you, and I am proud to say that, that is in my eyes the correct way of parenting and I will always be like that.

ALL THE PLANS YOUR MUM HAD FOR YOU WENT OUT THE WINDOW

What will happen to you when I sell up? I'd want to take you with me, your mum sees you as a trophy, and will she allow that to happen? Even though she knows it's for the best for you to be with me. I enrolled you into a nursery school in Chingford, my old school, this was because your mum showed no interest in trying to enrol you anywhere, in the past she made plans for you to go to a Catholic school, she was going to go to church so she could give you the best education, but then again why am I surprised this has not happened, am I drilling it into your head yet? You're a second thought to her. Anyways I mentioned it to your mum that I had plans to enrol you to my old school in December 2013 and she agreed because it would be easier as I would drop you off to your nene and she would take you to school and pick you up. But as soon as the day came that I told her that you would be starting nursery within a week, this is when her trophy mum status went into overdrive, and her dumb attitude came to light. I was asked why I never mentioned it to her, when in fact I had texts on my phone telling her what I was doing, but yet again I was being made to look like the fool, being made to look like a bad father for doing what she should have been doing.

Whatever I do good for you, your mum hates, especially if it's in front of special people like, teachers, doctors etc... She in front of these people wants to look important, wants to showcase a fifteen minute performance to show them how good a mum she is. I on the other hand hinge all my hope in you. I don't put on a performance, I let you show the world who your daddy is, unlike your mum who shows the world herself, to prove to the world and maybe to herself that she is a mum.

I DON'T NEED TO USE YOU TO SHOW THE WORLD I AM A DAD

It's the instance at the hospital where you had to stay overnight, although I took you to the doctors all the time, your mum was adamant she had to stay with you. Just like school, your nene and me set it all up, but your mum wanted to show she was around, even though her name was on the paperwork and believe me I really didn't want to do that, but I give her the respect she deserves even when at times I honestly don't think she deserves it. Your first day back from school you were given a book to read as homework, your mum made sure she wrote in the remarks page, not that it bothers me that she did, it's encouraging to see she read you the book, but what bothers me is that she had to sign it as mum when there was no need to write who read the book. This is all to show people its mum that's doing everything, or pretending its mum doing everything. It hurts me, because it shows she's trying to play games with me, but I won't react, I won't sign my name as dad at all, it doesn't matter who reads to you, as long as someone reads and you do your homework.

There are so many instances I could talk about, some I know I'll probably forget to mention, and this has literally just come to my mind. Just after Christmas Day in 2013, you developed a rash on your arms, I was at work, your mum was off as it was still part of her Christmas leave and was looking after you. She told me that you had been around her cousins kid that had got some illness, I believe it was foot and mouth disease and that I should get an appointment at the doctors, which I did, when it comes to you I act immediately. I was lucky to get an appointment for that day, I phoned your mum back telling her to take you to the doctors. Bear in mind we lived in Romford and the doctors surgery was in Chingford. Your mum said she wasn't prepared to travel to take you as her close cousin was round her mum's house, and that if I was so worried that I should take you. Well that's what I did, I left work, travelled from north London into Essex, to pick you up and drive all the way back to Chingford for you to be seen. I have to bite my tongue sometimes to her actions and thoughts, and the way she acts, yes she does it because she knows I will do anything for you, but you must realise, it's always been me that's been there for you, and everyone else must realise not all mums think of their kids first, and believe me after this experience I feel there a lot of people like your mum out there, and I am beginning to think there are a lot of fathers out there that are being used by their babies mothers.

YOUR MUMS NOT ALONE, THERE'S MANY LIKE HER OUT THERE

I work in a shop where I see single mothers coming in all day long, and you know what? I can now tell who is happy and who is not. I can tell who's a good mum and who is not, I can tell who cheats and who doesn't, I can even tell from a simple glance who uses the benefits scheme to their advantage, people like that make me sick, I could have easily been written off by the doctors on endless times, but I refuse to do so, I'm not a low life, I work hard for what I have, I have morals in life and with that in mind, it's a phrase that I will use on numerous occasions in this book, but I am able to look in the mirror and feel proud of who I am. Going back to the people I see, I from experience can actually now tell who fakes a smile just to be strong and show they are fine, because I am one of those people myself.

This story, if you haven't figured out has no priority order, so much has happened to me and at times in this book I've been unable to write them as and when they happened, but I'm writing them down in a way to tell you my story. When I say this I mean that the situations and the positions I have been put in to are not in any particular order from earliest to latest, why? Because this is a medium I am using to express my feelings to you, and whatever comes first is what comes out first, I'm also sure that there will be stories that have slipped my mind and are not included, I did eventually carry a little note book in my pocket everywhere I went, this was because the emotional state I was in, random thoughts of experiences I've had would just pop into my head and I had to note it down to help me write my story.

I DID GIVE UP, BUT NOW I WANT TO BE PROUD OF WHO I AM AGAIN

When this first happened to me, I did give up on life, not to the state that I just didn't do anything, but I was looking after you and working all the time, no time for friends and family, and in particular no time for me. I would go to bed at night and when I woke up I would sigh and feel disappointed that my circumstances were the same. What was I hoping for? Do I believe that all my problems will be resolved overnight? Then again the only problem I have is your mum, her attitude and actions made me never smile, in fact I cried behind closed doors all the time, tears that no one ever saw, silent tears my dear girl are the worst tears anyone can ever have. Please, I beg you, if you ever feel you can only cry when you are alone, please come and get a hug from me.

My teyze mentioned to my mum, because she must have noticed the downfall of me, why had I given up on life? I had apparently just stopped in my tracks and given up. That was true, my future was bleak, the smiles and jokes I had and did, were now gone. I was beginning to get too serious with life and everything around me was just building up stress levels within me, little did I know the stress was going to make me ill.

I couldn't see a future, I thought about what my teyze had said, was I waiting to die? Maybe, maybe I was.

I went to two family parties with you; one was for my cousins daughters six month henna party, the other was for my cousins wedding. On both these occasions I felt like I was suffocating, I felt like the whole room was caving in on me. To best describe the way I was feeling is to say I felt claustrophobic, I had family members coming up to me mentioning how proud they were with me and most men in my shoes would have gave up, they told me to continue the good work on how I was bringing you up. Yes, it was nice to hear those comments, but all they saw was the strong side of me, they never saw the weak side of me, the one side that was itching to win the battle. But hearing those comments should have boosted my confidence, it should have made me feel good inside, but instead it made me feel worse, it actually made me realise that my whole family were talking about me behind my back, I didn't want to be the centre of attention, especially for this reason. Maybe that's why I felt claustrophobic, because I thought everyone was looking and talking about me. What had happen to me? I rarely saw my family and since the arrival of your mum into my life I never saw them, what was worse was that I didn't want to be around them at a time of celebration, I wanted to leave and go home with you and leave them to it.

I FELT CLAUSTROPHOBIC

What was the real reason of me wanting to leave? Was it because I didn't want to be around my family who knew everything or was it because of where we were? We were present in an atmosphere that should be happy and have a celebration feel, that sort of atmosphere is something I can't do anymore, it just doesn't feel right and it's not my natural instinct no more, however I would say me wanting to leave was a combination of the two reasons.

As I now write this bit your three years and five months old, I've dropped you off at nursery and the three hours I have now before I pick you up are the only three hours in the week I have no work, no you, no family, just me. I use this time so I can reflect on what my life is, but understand due to the importance of my job there are also times that these three hours must be used for me to go to work to finish off bits I don't have time to do when I'm actually at work. At the moment I write this, I'm sitting with a cup of coffee in a well known coffee shop, with my laptop in front of me. These are the little things in life that are so precious that we take for granted, my free time is worth so much.

As I read back what I wrote, I feel I need to explain why I said maybe, to when I asked am I waiting to die? Because there's times that I feel it's the only way out for me from the hell hole your mum is making of my life. Again, don't be alarmed of what I write now; I've never been crazy, just angry and emotional. However there's times when the limited time I have to myself gets to me, everything builds up and my thoughts go insane, I've always had this thing where I talk to myself, always running through events and circumstances in my mind, going through every scenario and conversation that may happen, and I'd be a fool if I never admitted how life would be if I just died, again I'd never ever kill myself because I'd know the heartache you would grow up to have and it wouldn't be fair on you. But the scenarios can get too real at times, such as when I'm driving and a thought comes to mind if I have an accident, the thoughts end up having me in tears and that's because the first thought after this would be that I would never see or hear you again. I never ever want to upset you, if what you read does, I am so sorry, but one day maybe you'll fully understand why I am saying these things, maybe one day you'll get the point.

I NEVER WANT THIS STORY TO UPSET YOU

Just writing that statement brings tears to my eyes, and I'm not just writing that. If I can't or don't see you for a day, if I can't give you that goodnight kiss and cuddle or that trademark morning slap in my face from you to wake me up, may I add you do kiss me straight after the slap, without that it would really ruin my day, you're like my caffeine that keeps me going, you're like the reason I have for doing things to keep me going on and on and on and on. Your mum on the other hand, she'll be more than happy not to see you or make contact with you, she's been off to Egypt on numerous occasions now, and to be honest I've lost count on the actual number of times.

Although she hides the fact she goes away, it's obvious she goes to see her boyfriend who is more important. She's told lies such as she's going Alton towers with her cousin, to the point of saying her work is taking her South Africa to see suppliers, to even a lie that she is going Cornwall for the weekend, which turns out to be five nights because I text to find out if she could pick you up one day, as I had to stay late at work, to which I got a reply "no I told you I wasn't coming back until Wednesday", however I had the text from her on my phone which said that she was going away for the weekend, either way it really doesn't bother me, but I think she thinks it does.

I DON'T CARE WHERE YOUR MUM GOES, OR WHO WITH

It's got to the stage that she now pulls off luggage straps off the suitcase to prove she hasn't gone nowhere as I caught her out on this before, but as clueless as your mum is, she leaves a receipt on the tumble dryer in the kitchen from Luton airport with a flight number on it to Egypt, as well as sometimes wearing a new Egyptian t-shirt, does your mum think I'm actually stupid? When I actually question why she lied where she went, as usual she gets defensive and tells me why I'm nosing around and that it's none of my business.

Now this bit may hurt you, but it needs to be told, but the fact that she's happy to spend as little as ten minutes with you as a mum, but she can't spend a day from not talking to her boyfriend, Skyping or doing whatever, in fact she shows more tears of missing her boyfriends then she does for not seeing you. There is this one occasion which I think is appropriate, the day before one of her travels to Egypt which she didn't lie to me about, she was going to go with her cousin, now her passport went missing. It's no surprise your mum accused me of taking it and hiding it, in her head I did it because I didn't want her to go. What a joke! In fact I wanted her to go, and I actually started to help her look for it, to which I got a reply, "you think you're clever pretending to help me when you've taken it". Your mum cried that day, I've never seen her cry for you ever, but I've now seen her cry because she couldn't go to Egypt, she thought she was not going to be able to see her boyfriend and spend precious time with him.

Your mum even started questioning you if you had seen her silly passport, but you were clueless, your mum was adamant she put it in the front zip of her suitcase. She eventually found it in her bed, to which she then mysteriously remembered that she had it and was looking at it a couple of nights prior. No surprise your mum never apologised for accusing me, but then again, I really wasn't expecting it, I was glad she found it so me and you could have a break from her. After reading this, all I will add is where do her priorities lie? Ten minutes with your daughter, a whole evening, night, and probably endless calls and texts throughout the day with someone who should never come close to you, tears for your boyfriend over your daughter, it just shows who and what makes her more happy.

I NEED TO GET A LIFE APPARENTLY

I tried to question your mum on this once, the response I got was, go get a life, just because I have one, like all the other times, I gave no response, I just sighed and thought to myself, my life is my daughter, you're the one who needs to get a life.

When your mum went to Egypt, I sometimes wondered how she felt, she showed no emotion towards you, on leaving or on a return, yeah she brought you a gift once, a gift from South Africa apparently, because that's where work had taken her to see the suppliers, I knew she went to Egypt but she is adamant she never. My mind works in wondrous ways, the gift she brought you was a Middle Eastern purse with some plastic bracelets which to me looked like an Egyptian feel more then the South African feel, which proved to me where your mum had been. I don't actually care where your mum goes, in fact I prefer when she's not around, you never play up, you listen to every word I say, you do everything I ask you to do, when your mums around, you use the word "no" a lot, you run around not wanting to do things. At first I thought maybe it's me, but I saw the truth to why you play up. At first when you told me, I ignored it because I thought you were making little stories up, you used to tell me "mummy smack me". One day I saw it with my own eyes, your mum told you that she was going to put you to bed, we seem to have this tantrum from you every time she puts you to bed, you always say "no, I want daddy", but on this occasion you had a plastic toy golf club in your hand, and when your mum angrily told you that she was going to do it, you threw the golf club on the floor and it rebounded near your mums foot.

HOW DARE SHE DO THAT TO YOU?

I stayed silent to what I saw; I actually wanted to grab your mum and throw her out the house and tell her to never touch my daughter again. She got up, she shouted at you, which followed a hard smack on your bum. I was fuming inside, what was she doing? She grabbed you and took you to the stairs and told you to sit down. You were screaming for me, crying out for me, I sat still, I didn't look at your mum or I think I would have exploded, I think I would have gone mad at her, instead I looked into my bowl of food that I was trying to eat. I was hungry when I made it, I only had two spoon full's, and I was now choking on what I didn't want to eat anymore.

Instead of your mum talking to you and telling you what you had done wrong, she was resulting into using physical ways to tell you off. You had previously started using this sort of behaviour towards your mum, sometimes me and you're nene; it was clear where you had picked it up from. Eventually after a lot of crying and screaming and the fact you began to gasp for air because you were now trying to make yourself sick I had to get involved. I hate seeing you have tears, I hate seeing you scared because that's what I could see in your eyes and I could tell from the way you were calling out for me. I told your mum to let you come to me, she wouldn't have it, I told her to let me deal with it, there's ways to deal with issues like this, you talk to them, you don't scare them not to do things. You just wanted to cuddle me, and I understood why, but I had to ease you off as I sat you down, got down to your level and asked what you had done wrong, told you to tell mummy you was sorry to which you did, and I did eventually calm you down.

I always said and do say if anyone touched my daughter I would hurt them back, but this is your mum, the position I am in, I can't because if I do, I'll end up losing you, and believe me, after seeing what I had seen there and then, you need me more than ever or I truly believe that you will become one of those kids I hate, one of those naughty kids without respect or care of others and the world if your mum had to look after you all the time.

NO ONE HAS THE RIGHT TO HIT MY CHILD, NOT EVEN ME

I'm sorry on many counts as a father, I'm sorry you'll never have the normal father every child has, most children, most of your friends won't come from broken families and I know it will upset you when they describe of how they did things as a family, a holiday, a trip to the beach, a simple birthday party or even an evening to the restaurant. I'm sorry I couldn't keep your mum on our side, I'm sorry that maybe I didn't do enough which I don't think is possible but I'm sorry because it's for you, but and this is a big but, and a positive but, you have a father beyond any normal father and that my dear girl is something you should be very proud of, because no normal child will have that, that much I can and will promise you with all my heart. I've slightly told this story to a few people, only bits here and there, and majority of them believe I am talking crap, they believe I make up things because apparently fathers can't be like me, they can't keep doing the things I do, one even laughed and asked if I was Superman. This whole bubble in this country or even the world of how mums are the main parent and should have full responsibility really annoys me to such a point that I just walk away from people saying this or I will look like a disruptive father putting his point out that no one will believe.

People saying mums should have their children not fathers, mums having more rights are statements from people who need to wake up and understand that some kids are better off with their dad. You and I are living proof that what people say don't count, just like I will always fight for you, and I promise you I will, if you want something, and it's that important to you, and there are ways of getting it, and by all means, anything is possible, maybe this story is a start to get realisation out into the world.

PEOPLE NEED TO UNDERSTAND THAT A DAD CAN BE MORE POWERFUL THAN A MUM

When your mum originally left to live with your nanny, yes I struggled with the thought that you had gone and I didn't see you every day, yes I made choices to take you to nene and return you, but that was because of me wanting to see you and make sure you was ok, but my spare time when I was away from you was hard, and for me I tried to make our home, a home. I decorated your room, I rearranged it, the spare room I was going to make into an office, but as I've already said your mum returning the way she did, and what she did to turn my world even more upside down was reason enough to stop. I gave up hope, I lost interest in the house, cleaning went out the window; I had no pride in the house that should have been called home. Your mum would eat my stuff without asking, I couldn't be bothered to shop. I began to shop daily because that's what it came to; I was washing your mum's dishes because I couldn't move in the kitchen. The living room became your mum's as she wouldn't budge from the moment she got in to watch her programmes as well as to talk to her boyfriends. Your bedroom became hers and yours and the real reason to why you didn't want to sleep there, as you would tell me you don't want mummy in your room. The spare room became a walk in closet for your mum, as I said I lost hope and pride, DIY went out the window I just couldn't be bothered anymore. I haven't got a home, I'm writing this, and I don't know where my home is anymore, just like you when you tell me you don't want to go home, just like you when you see your mum's car when we pull up outside the house, I don't want to go in, and I know from the frown upon your face, and the tone of your voice when you say "mummy's here" that you don't want to go in either. All I want in life is to give you a home, a life that you will be happy with, I want you to grow up to be a proper princess, I want to give you all the happiness in the world, but I can't because your mum keeps getting in the way. Now there will come a time when I will sell the house, you're mum will demand a share of it, as in her own words aimed towards me, she told me if I had to move on with my life I had to pay her off, she keeps telling me she had my kid and I needed to pay for that. You're mum don't deserve anything, she really has put nothing in to it, but maybe I'll be able to start a fresh and build a home for you again, but there's something that will kill me so much, I know leaving and selling the home we don't want, it will test our bond, the bond that's got even stronger since your mums return to the house because I've seen you every day, and our bond may fade with our absence and that is something I am terrified of. I won't see you every day, I won't kiss you goodnight every night, I won't know your safe and I won't hear your cries for me, so as previously promised by daddy, I won't always be there for you because someone will stop that for selfish reasons.

It will kill me not seeing you every day

Even at this moment of time, even with your mum in our face in a house she is not welcomed in, it's still me that dresses you in the mornings whilst your mum has a bath, and puts all her make up on. It's me that takes you to nene, picks you up after work, and ninety percent of the time it's me that puts you to bed. On Sundays both your mum and me are off, and still it's me that looks after you all day long, on the rare occasion your mum may take you out, but that's because she will be going around her family and she won't have the responsibility of looking after you, as she will know that others will cause a fuss to see you, as I have called it, a trophy mum moment. Even on my days off, I take you to nursery, once I've dropped you off, I just wait for you to finish as there is no point coming back home as your school is in Chingford where all my family are. No matter how much I struggle, I wouldn't change it for the world, as everything I do is for you, and by doing this and thinking this I always know it's all worthwhile.

EVERYTHING I DO IS FOR YOU

All the people that have told me to stand up for myself, told me to speak up should realise if I do, I'm the one that will be made to look bad. It got me thinking, everything in this house is mine, or paid for by me, as long as I don't put you out, maybe I can prove a point to your mum that I want to sell, and I want her out, because when I mentioned to her I wanted to leave she told me she had nowhere to go, not that I care where she goes, but she uses you as a reason I can't sell up saying that I will put you out if I do sell up. So as I said, maybe it's time I played some games, I can't afford to pay bills all the time, I hardly watch TV, so why do I pay for Satellite TV, I can instantly kill her relationship with this Egyptian guy by cutting off the internet, but unfortunately I need the internet for my own work related tasks. Something I have started and will continue is that when she doesn't wash dishes and leaves them by the side, I just throw them in a bin bag and bin them the next day when I'm out and about. I know it's a petty thing I'm doing, some may even say rather childish, but I'm tired and annoyed of the games and laziness of this self centred girl and it is all now getting to me. Maybe it's time for me to prove a point, by throwing these things away, the only person that's out of pocket is me, I paid for them, it's not like I'm throwing her stuff away, so she really has no say to what I do to my own things. Your mum did ask at first when she realised the kitchen was getting bare, she asked where all the dishes, cutlery and cups had gone? I was honest, I said when you don't wash them, I throw them away! She called me crazy and insane; no surprise there to be honest, but she also tried to convince me that she did do the washing, but believe me, I give her all night to wash them, when I get up in the morning and they're still there, I'm sorry but she had her time to wash them, especially when all I hear is her talking on the phone to her boyfriend for long periods of time, if that didn't take up her time it would be the TV that would take it all up.

THERE'S A BIG DIFFERENCE BETWEEN REGRET AND SORRY

After reading all this, you may find it hard to believe that to date, I have never ever received or heard the word sorry from your mum, she has told me that she regrets doing what she did, this is during the time that she wanted us to get back together, but she has never ever said sorry for what she did. Maybe it's my over thinking or just my issue that I over analyse things. I broke down the two words, sorry to me means you genuinely care about hurting the other person, in my position for what she had put my mental state through, but then I thought about what regret meant. That's the point where I kind of put your mum's mental state and her thinking into place, it made sense. Regret to me means that you made a decision or an action which didn't benefit yourself, no feeling sorry for anyone, only person that could be felt sorry for when you regret doing something is yourself. Just think about it, I'm sorry I did that, or I regret doing that. The words we choose to use are a clever way of who we are, and secretly disguise what we want to say.

Another example that rages my fury and adds fuel to the anger within me is an instant where I came home from work late one evening, as I was doing a changeover, your mum was on the sofa as I noticed the big mirror from the hall way taken off the wall, my first thought was that it fell and broke as your mum liked to place you above the top of the radiator which is where this mirror was situated and get you to jump into her arms. Anyways all I did was ask what happened to the mirror? Her selfish and rude response was, "well my mirrors broken, and its part of the house so it's mine".

I was fuming inside, but I kept calm, I told your mum I used that mirror, which I did, but more importantly I reminded her, the mirror she broke was not one that she brought, in fact it was the mirror I brought for the bedroom that I slept in.

This is proof again that your mum don't spend money on things she should, in fact all her money goes on is holidays to see her boyfriend, and clothes etc.

NEVER EVER BE SELFISH OR SELF CENTRED

I told your mum she was selfish, that evening the living room was a mess, dishes had not been done again, and I had been on my feet all day again and on a day in which should have been my day off as I normally have Sundays off, your mum went upstairs and went to bed. I cleaned the living room and did the dishes, whilst doing the dishes I noticed I didn't wash a medicine spoon, you had been poorly and been prescribed medication by the doctor. I know she failed to give you any medicine the day before even after I reminded her, and again reminded her on this day before I left to go work. I checked the medicine in the fridge as soon as I noticed no spoon and it was the same amount as I left it, as I knew how much was in the bottle as it was me that gave you your medicine in the morning when you woke up.

I questioned your mum, why she didn't give you medicine, she said she did, when I told her she didn't because there was no medicine spoon that needed washing, she felt the need to lie again and say she washed the spoon. So she leaves everything else to be washed but washes one little spoon, I think not as the washing on the rack was the washing that I had done again prior to me leaving for work in the morning.

My question is what did your mum do all day? The day before again I was at work and it being a Saturday your mum had you all day, I walked into no washing being done, the living room a mess and my bedroom like a robbery had been committed. Your mum does whatever she wants when she wants, and there really is no easing up from her end, this just shows she is just selfish. Just to add one more thing about that day, after your mum got out of bed at eleven in the morning, she wondered into the living room, switched the TV over and watched her own programmes. I thought the days of her ignoring you were over, but again you wanted to get your mums attention about the princess dress you were wearing, but she didn't flinch, she just stared at the TV, even after you called for her as little as five times, and at a very loud voice as well. As I always do I told you to come and talk to me, the more she does this, the more you become mine, can't your mum see this?

SURELY YOUR MUM MUST HURT INSIDE

I know your mum must be hurt inside, if not I question your mum to why she is not; maybe your mum is not well, maybe she has mental issues which might be a reason to why she keeps branding me as being insane and crazy. How a child can be so close to one parent is nice for me, but if the tables were reversed I would be very upset. Now there are situations that happen or things your mum does that prove to me that she is hurting. Look, your used to daddy, and when your mum walked away we comforted each other and I allowed you to sleep in my bed so you felt safe and for me to realise why I was doing what I was doing was not for me but for you, now you got used to this, I understand you needed your bed and I brought you one, but the realisation is that you were a daddy's girl, you probably only feel safe with daddy around, so I moved your bed into my room as you wouldn't want to sleep in your own room. Now this to me was not an issue as I always had plans to ease you into your room. On your mum's return she allowed your bed to remain in my room, until the day of your third birthday, she arranged to have a party inside our house for her family, it's safe to say when things like this happen I disappear, I am forced out my home or house, she invites her cousins, her family to my home, she invites her friends, when I don't have any; no way am I having my mates or family come round, I feel embarrassed of what's happened to me, your mum must feel proud of what she has done, boasting what she is and who she is.

IS YOUR MUM ACTUALLY PROUD OF WHO SHE IS?

Anyways the eve of your third birthday without asking me she dragged your bed out of my room and put it back in your room, the same room in which she slept on a mattress, I didn't question it because I knew it was right, but the truth was that she didn't want her family to realise that you were truly a daddy's girl, she didn't want them to realise that daddy did all the work, she wanted to give her own family a false image that mummy was the one who did most if not all. Your bed going back into your room, especially a room in which your mum slept in was a big mistake, because it just caused you more reasons to get upset but also caused me more reasons to stress inside. You would wake up in the middle of the night, the times would vary, and your first thought would be daddy, you would run out the room and jump into my bed in the other room, this would last a very long time, don't get me wrong there's nights you stayed in my bed from the start because you would put up a fuss or because your mum would just allow you to, then these are the nights I realised that the light for your room would remain on, and that she would be talking with someone, your guess is probably better than mine on what she was up to, but more than likely she was probably on Skype, why else would the lights remain on?

You know that there are even occasions whilst you slept in your bed she would still talk on her phone, if I can hear your mum talking from my room, surly you could hear her as well as you would be right next to her. You're only little, you really don't deserve to be treated this way, why can't your mum take her phone call downstairs where she wouldn't be bothering you whilst you sleep? How is any of all this fair on you? As I've said on numerous occasions, I've given up talking to your mum because her replies are worthless, and it will just anger me up to the point my stress levels would build up and I would probably do something to hurt her that would put me in trouble. If I did say something, your mum would probably just reply on the lines of that I'm jealous because people want to talk to her and no one wants to talk to me.

IF I DID WHAT YOUR MUM DID AND DOES, I'D HAVE YOU TAKEN AWAY FROM ME

I encouraged you to sleep in your bed, but when you looked at me and told me you wanted to sleep with me, I always used to reply the same thing, I used to tell you that in the morning when you woke up, you could come and have some cuddles, this is when you told me that your mum told you that you weren't allowed to come to daddy any more, and that she hurt you. Again at the time I didn't believe your mum would be that extreme, I thought you were just making it sound worse then it was, why would your mum hurt you? That's until one night I heard you crying saying you wanted daddy, I heard your mum in her angry yet quiet voice, probably quiet so I couldn't hear, she was telling you that you weren't allowed and for you to get in her bed and not to come to me. I remember you screaming your hurting me, you somehow got away and came into my room and cuddled up to me, I asked if you were ok, you said mummy grabbed your arm and wouldn't let you go. It hurts me to write this, it hurts me that I've never told anyone but my own mum, it hurts me that if I say things like this in public I will always be seen as the bad guy because I'm the dad and not the mum. Seriously if a dad was doing the things that your mum does, the dad would be locked away by now or their child would be taken away from them.

I believe your mum began to get a little clever after that, maybe those occasions you screaming and running to dad in the night were what she needed to wake her up, and hit her emotions. She sparingly started to put you to bed, she used to ask if you wanted mummy cuddles or want to watch songs on her ipad, it was all little techniques to get you into her bed, what really got to me, was that she would moan if you slept with me on occasions but for her to do it in your room on her mattress with the door closed so I wouldn't find out was wrong, there's ways of trying to get your love, not by making daddy the bad guy, not by making me seem like I didn't want you. I know that's what she tries to do behind closed doors, I just have this feeling, but I draw the line on playing games with you, if I do it will confuse you, instead I let my love for you do the talking, and I am sure that this will be enough.

"DADDY DON'T GO"

Love between a father and in my case a daughter is so special, and the simplest things are the best. On one occasion I worked late, and your mum picked you up from nene, by the time I got back you were asleep in your bed room, anyways you woke up at around half eleven, you came running into my room, you realised I was in bed as I was watching TV, you got yourself in to my bed, you just stared at my face, you started smiling and at the same time you told me you loved me and that you wanted a kiss, you held my hand and told me "Daddy don't go" and you fell asleep in my arms whilst you held my hand. That night I just cried and to be honest, I know men aren't suppose to own up to things like this but since your birth and since what I've been through I have become so emotional it's unreal. I know our bond will forever get tested, people will try and break it, but you know what? I now know that our bond will never break, there was times when your mum first left I got scared that you would never know about our bond, but as long as I'm healthy and so are you, nothing will stand in our way.

IT WAS THE DREAM THAT WOULD CHANGE MY OUTLOOK ON LIFE FOREVER

It's amazing that I've just wrote that our bond will never break, but what's more amazing is that I had a dream, well maybe more a nightmare then a dream because I saw our bond possibly come to a near end, and that image I saw has seriously changed the outlook I've had on life. What I saw was a dream that changed my outlook on everything I do, it made me realise that my priorities in life are sometimes in the wrong places where I put work before family, friends etc. Where I work too hard, where your mum is in my face twenty four seven which stops me moving forward with my life, and in saying that my life is now in need of moving forward, forward with you of course. So what was this dream, it's a dream that was situated in my bedroom as I lay asleep on my bed, looking on from the end of the bed was another me, it was clear that the image looking on was a ghost or spirit figure and the body in the bed of me was not asleep, in fact it was clear I was dead, you then suddenly ran into the room as you always did, jumped into bed to wake me up, but you was unable to, you began to cry and slap my face to get me to wake up as you shouted "WAKE UP DADDY, WAKE UP". Now if that was the entire dream I would say fine, it was just a dream, but the fact that I woke up from my sleep with you slapping my face and telling me to wake up is scary. You that evening had fallen asleep on my bed and I didn't want to move you to your bed as you looked really comfortable. When I woke up, you just put your head back on the pillow and slept, I on the other hand couldn't, I was scared, emotionally tearful, I stayed awake just thinking of what had happened had meant. I told your hala about it, she told me that she could relate to how scary seeing yourself dead in your sleep is, but also said that maybe you was only slapping me in the face because I could have been calling out for help or shouting in my sleep and I woke you up. I know this may sound like a shrink job, but seriously this dream has turned my life upside down, I'm ready to walk away from work now, ready to throw my keys at my boss.

READY TO THROW MY KEY'S AT MY BOSS

This became near reality soon after that dream when I had agreed to go and collect you from school so I could see you because I was to work late one evening, again due to a changeover, it's at that moment at about ten past three in the afternoon where I was to leave my store to come to you when my boss walked in to do a visit. Now my store, and I will be the first to admit that it had been wrecked from a busy day's trade and also due to limited stock due to us changing it around that evening. I was told off for it, but what made it worse was that my bosses boss also turned up to give me more grief, I was so close to just walking out, I was being given grief, not in as many words but I was called lazy along with my team, when in fact we don't get a break, don't get time to drink a sip of water let alone go toilet as and when needed. They say the work life in retail is hard, over worked, and under paid, but add being the best dad in the world to that, you realise just how tired and stressed I may feel at times.

I felt like I let you down, I told you that morning I was to pick you up; instead I phoned your nene pleading to pick you up because I had to stay at work. I sometimes think my family feel I use work as an excuse because I'm always saying that I am working, but seriously its tough doing what I do, and I plead you never get into this industry, it's the only thing I don't want you to follow your dad in.

WORK JUST GOT MORE INTENSE

My work since me and your mum broke up has got more intense, more commitment is required, staff hours keep getting cut and expectations and standards are greater than before. I personally as I write this don't feel like a manager, instead I feel like an overworked and underpaid individual who is on less then minimal wage if you calculated the amount of hours

I do. I am unable to look for another job because of my current personal situations with you being the main priority in my life; no other job will accept the demands I have. I'm very lucky that the store I run, the people I have allow me to do the hours I do so I can be there for you whenever you need me most. No matter how annoyed or frustrated I am at work, I will never give up, I will always give one hundred percent of the best of my ability. Just like everything in life, when the pressure is on, when time is of the essence, you will eventually begin to take short cuts, and with my immense commitments from outside of work, I began to rush things such as paperwork, by doing this I was given two red audits, and a written warning to top it all off. I won't argue with what was sanctioned, but I'm tired, there's only so much one person can do. I've always sang the song that you don't bring your problems to work, I never wanted to, I try to lock them away before I enter my store, I've never wanted them to combine, but they have. Your mum has turned my life upside down in more ways then you or anyone could ever imagine.

YOUR MUM COMBINED MY PERSONAL AND WORK LIFE INTO ONE

Following your dad is something you like doing, and I enjoy seeing you do it. Yes you always run after me etc, but I'm more on about following the things I do, you enjoy cooking with me, you enjoy writing just like me, if I go to make a list for instance for shopping, you too want a piece of paper and pen so you can create your own list so we can take it to the supermarket. Now this might make you giggle, but when I ask you what is on your list, depending on your mood, you may say strawberries, sugar, flour, eggs, but it always ends with toys. I do need to say this mind, when we do go shopping, you are so good, you understand I won't buy you everything you want, you tend to understand I will buy you one thing and one thing only, you understand if I say it's too much money and you put it away but you are such a good girl and will always only choose one thing. If you then change your mind and want something else, you will always say put this back and give me this, my angel you are so clever and understanding, you truly are an angel sent from above for me.

SHE'S NOT A BOY

Following my footsteps depending on how you look at it is a good thing; something which I am confident you are, and probably makes me smile is that you are a Gunner. For your third birthday I introduced you to Arsenal, I brought you your first football kit with your name and the number six on it, complete with shirt, shorts, socks and proper football boots. I was in two minds if you would like it, but because I had my own kit, you wanted it, and you soon began to memorise the badge belonging to Arsenal. You will now wherever possible, wherever you see the badge, you will shout out Arsenal, daddies little girl hey. The kit had mixed reviews, my family and friends thought it was amazing, your mum on the other hand, her reply was simple, "she's not a boy", but as I said your mum will never ever appreciate what I do for you, whatever I do is wrong, but it's also the bond we have that she don't get, she don't get its more to do then football, it's something we share an interest with, because you do share an interest in it, you love to kick a ball, and I am adamant you are two footed, you kick with both your left and right foot, now that's a skill that not many can boast about, maybe you learnt through the games we played together when you grew up.

PLAYING GAMES WITH YOU AND SEEING YOU LEARN IS NOW THE BEST THING I DO

As sad as this may sound, I began to show you some of my old TV programs I used to watch when I was growing up as you asked what daddy use to watch as a baby. I thought you would say something on the terms of turn it off, but you enjoyed watching the likes of Button Moon, Dog Tanian, Poddington Peas, Gummy Bears, when you watch them, you ask if I watched them as a baby, when I said yes, you would lay in my lap and watch them and say that you're watching daddy's baby cartoons.

The little people that know I am writing this book, they have asked why I'm doing such a thing, one even said, your daughters going to hate you for telling her your story. In my head I'm thinking if I was my daughter I'd have a completely different outlook then you, I'd be thinking my dad is being truthful, all he is doing is saying what's happened, but deep down I would also be thinking that if this didn't happen to him, then he wouldn't need to write anything, and I know I'd have immense pride if my dad left me a story to explain everything. I'd also not blame him for the truth, it's the person or things or circumstances that led him to write his story. But please don't blame anyone, and don't ever hate or blame your mum, I am sure in due course your mums thoughts and her own actions will haunt her for the rest of her life. Your mum lost everything not for herself, but for you, I won't be there for her when it happens, but I plead you will, family means more to me than anything and you having a near normal family is still a wish I hold and have for you.

HAVE PRIDE IN THIS BOOK

Only time will tell what the future holds, what the future holds for your mum is something in which I really don't care for. As for me I've put my life on hold since your mum returned, the search for my sole partner came to an end, I just gave up looking. I deserve the best, but whilst your mum interferes in my life and in my space, no worthy girl will ever understand. Yes I get lonely, I get annoyed all the time that my life is stuck and this is all because of your mum. I won't just accept anyone, they need to meet my standards, and as selfish as I may sound now, I want someone to want me for who I am, for who we are.

I want someone to fight for me, to look after me; I really deserve someone with these qualities. I hope the future is better then what it is now, but my priority is that your life is not hindered in anyway; I hope you are a happy child and enjoy everything that comes your way. I will do everything I can to make sure of that, so that is made possible.

I DESERVE SOMEONE WHO WANTS ME FOR WHO I AM, AND UNDERSTANDS MY PAST

I am also aware your mum will never get off my back; I know she will never leave me alone, it's sad to say but she will never make it easy for me even when she isn't living with me. You see I know your mum better then she knows herself, and I know in the future when I do find that girl I can love, and a girl we can both trust, your mum will be there to interfere. I also know, whatever changes I may make or do to benefit me or you in our life, your mum will also be there to interfere to put a stop to it. She will use you the way she always does to put my life on hold. I know why she does it, and I know why she will continue to do it forever, she won't accept that I can have a better life without her, she won't be able to accept that my life will be better than her own, she won't ever stop comparing my life to hers, and if my life will seem better than her own, she will up her game and use you to get at me. She knows you're the only person, the only thing I cherish so much that I will stop at an instant to make sure you are fine. Why would she be that evil? Because she wants people to look at her, wants people to see how clever she is, and if she broke up a family for no good reason, people will start asking her questions to why she has, especially when people will start telling her you lost him, you lost your family, for what? It's all an ego thing for your mum, nothing will ever be bigger than her, unfortunately that means you as well, and she only uses you to boost her own ego and popularity.

After writing so much of my past, it's been very upsetting for me to re-live many painful moments; these I know are moments and memories that I will never forget. Yes I have many questions that I will never get answers for, that much I know. Yes I know I will go to my grave a tired and hurt man, but I will be a very proud dad of what I have in the form of you, and that will be my last thought, and not the moments that put sad tears in my eyes.

YOU WILL BE MY LAST THOUGHT

If I could ever get an answer to any of my questions that run through my head, it would be this. Why? Why did your mum do the things she did. If she was never ready to be a mum to you and was never ready to be a future wife to me, why did she make me move away from my family and friends? Why did she make my life hell by making me work so hard to provide for you and to look after you as she just did nothing? Why has your mum no heart or soul? Why does she not respect me, and even you? Why does your mum not respect herself? I know I'll never get the true answers, I know even you will never get the true answers; I don't even think your mum knows the true answers. As I said it's all about your mum, it's all about her and what she wants and what she needs, she will do it as and when she wants and does not care who gets hurt along the way, I believe that's what being selfish and self centred is all about.

You have now read the story, a story that has been written for you, the story isn't complete yet, I have no idea how the story will end or develop, but the story needs to begin to change direction. If you were not here, and then believe me this story would not exist, but as you do, this is for you. No one has the right to question you about this book, and you have the right to give no answers. No one has the right to question me, some I know will call me soft for allowing what has happened happen, but you know what, it's their opinion, not mine and it's not yours unless you think it is, but also no one has the right to question your mum, she is your mum and no matter how much I as a person hate her, she is your mum, she may be judged but never questioned or hated. I'm going to write this bit into the book, just to show you how much I hate your mum, for me as a human being, as a normal person, I wish your mum would have a fatal accident, a painful accident, but then the only person that would be happy is me, and then I would look at you and see you unhappy, a little girl without her mum, and my priority in life is you, so as a father and not a human being, and being a father is more important, I would rather your mum was around. Maybe now you can understand why I don't react and why I let your mum just get on with things, it's all for you, and not for me.

IT'S HORRIBLE TO WHAT I SAY, BUT ITS HOW I FEEL

I have never wanted anyone to be dead, not even my worst enemies; it just shows how much your mum has got to me. I know that me saying that about your mum must upset you, but it's the truth and I am not going to lie to you, or cover up any truth to make me look like a saint, we all make mistakes in life, we all have thoughts and we all have our own actions, I've told you the truth and it's up to you what you do with it, you're mum made mistakes, some big mistakes, but she refuses to move on with them, and holds me back all the time. If your mum ever reads this book, this bit is for her. I owe you nothing, I gave you everything anyone could ever want, it's not my fault you never wanted it or wanted more, so now do me a favour and get out my life and let me move on, I don't need to look after you, the only person that needs my looking after is our daughter and that is it, and I will never neglect her, so stop your game playing and move on and accept the mistakes you have made in life.

Some will say I've written this book to bring your mum down, to try and get revenge, to try and get you to hate her, as I said as a human being there is nothing more I would like then that to happen, nothing more pleasing then to see you stick up your middle finger at her and tell her where to get off for what she has done to us both, but as a father that's the worst thing that could ever happen, and that's the last thing I want to ever happen. You have a right to know the truth, and I will argue with whoever tells me otherwise.

YOU HAVE THE RIGHT TO KNOW THE TRUTH

Just promise me one thing, I've grown up without my dad, I was never able to show him who I was or what I became, I was never able to make him proud of me and hear him tell me that he was of me. I've given your nene grief and strain although she's helped me a lot I can never ever show her just how grateful I am that she is my mum. Your mum is demanding and will take away some of the money my mum and dad left me, and I feel embarrassed that I am allowing this to happen. How can my parents be proud of me? I made a mistake in falling for someone and doing everything for someone who didn't and will never deserve it and I'm not just on about the money, I'm also talking about the time and effort I put into your mum. Your mum and her actions had put me to an all time low, there was a stage of my life prior to ever meeting your mum that I would go and see my dad's grave at least once a fortnight, as morbid as this may sound, in a hectic life it was nice to go and have a chat with him in calming surroundings. Even away from his grave at the cemetery, I'd sometimes talk to him through my mind, people say its crazy, but it's not, when you have respect for someone and you don't ever want to lose the love and memory of that person, they always will be by your side no matter what. Maybe with all your mum did to me, stopped all this, no lie since your mum began all these games, I haven't gone to my dad's grave once, and that grave is only a four minute drive from my workplace. I don't even speak to my dad any more, the only reason I can give you is that I am extremely embarrassed, and I know he can see everything I do, there is no way he would ever be proud of the decisions I made to be where I am now, especially when he worked so hard to try and give me a life that he wanted to, and that's the ethic that both he and my mum breathed, and that is the ethic I am trying to do for you.

All I've ever done in life is try to make my parents proud of me, and as a father I want you to be proud of me, a reason to why I have wrote this book. I hope one day you will try to make me proud of you just like I am now.

MAKE ME PROUD OF WHO YOU ARE

I believe no matter what you do in life I will always be proud of you, baring one thing. If you ever become like your mum, I will be distraught, I will not be happy, in fact I'll go to the point and say that everything I've done in my life to bring you up was a waste of time, and I wish I never bothered. I want you to respect people, and earn things yourself, don't treat people like fools, and never play mind games with anyone.

Again, why have I written this book? Because I want you to be proud of me, it's as simple as that, I don't want you to hate your mum, I don't want you to hold a grudge against her, I want your relationship with your mum to be strong, I only have one true goal and dream to come from this book, and that is that on my death bed you will be there to hold my hand. Just like my dad had his children by his death bed, just like many parents do in this world, but some sadly die alone. As horrible and cruel as this may sound, when I'm about to die I want you to be sad, because tears of pain show how important someone is to them, I should know as I cry for you every day of my life. On my death bed I want you to kiss me, tell me how proud you are of me, I want you to tell me you believe in hero's because I am your hero, and that you are thankful for everything I have done for you and that I am the best dad you could ever imagine, that you are the luckiest girl in the world and that my loss will leave a massive void in your life. Hearing that will allow me to fade away and it will allow me to rest in peace, something that I truly deserve to do, but knowing that everything I have ever done, all the hard work, all the stress that I went through was worth it and appreciated by the one person it was all done for, to hear you tell me that, will make me the happiest dad in the world.

Yes I know that I will miss you when I'm gone, and I know you will miss me, but that's what love is about, this is what love does.

I KNOW IT WAS ALL WORTH WHILE

Why should I hold everything back, should every emotion and thought I have be kept locked away inside me, why should people not have the right to understand who I am, and why I am like I am, why shouldn't I have the option to become that someone I used to be. Should I not have the right to speak out and fight back, for both of us? If your mum is so right in all her decisions then let her tell the world her story, get her to tell the world why she made every decision that has destroyed your dad to the brink that death seemed like the only answer out of this grey hole. You my dear baby girl were the sun, my angel that pulled me out that hole and gave me courage and realisation to be able to breath and to speak out. You gave me that little energy, that focus, to write this story, gave me belief that your love is all I need in this world, made me realise not to give in, and let your mum walk over me, writing and reading my story its allowed me to see what a fool I have been, how gullible and stupid I have been, but when you love someone, you will take all the grief and stress that comes with it, and when I said when you love someone, I know you knew I meant you because you're the only person I've done this for and no one else.

I WANT TO FIGHT BACK

My story and you are exactly what I needed to begin my fight back, this story will be the beginning of that fight back, to gain my respect from the people who lost faith in me, and that faith that I want won back is beginning with me, I want to respect myself again, I want to remember who I was before I met your mum. I was someone who was not afraid of the world and what it can be. This story is the start of your dad coming back, coming back to live his life, coming back to make a life for you and me. Believe me, if I was told I'd have to go through what I have been through again, I'd walk away now, I'd throw myself in the sea, it's been the hardest struggle I have ever been through and I hope I ever will. There's times what I've felt, what I've had to deal with was near impossible, people, normal people would have crumbled. There's nothing worse than false promises, nothing worse than being betrayed over and over again.

So why should I hold back, I have feelings, you need to know, and I don't care if strangers or friends and even family think my story shouldn't be told to you, I really don't care, I'm your dad, and we have been through things together that no one knows about. No one told me how to be a dad, it was my instinct of how to be one, no one taught me how to love you, no one taught me how to care for you, no one taught me how to cuddle you, or give you a kiss, no one taught me how to build a strong bond with you, I did all this on my own, so no one has the right to tell me what I can and can't tell you, I'm your dad, I will always be there, I've always been there, I've never neglected you and never will, I only do what's best for you.

No one knows you better than me, and funnily enough I don't think no one knows me better than you, even at such a tender young age.

NO ONE TAUGHT ME HOW TO BE A DAD

Who knows when my time will be up, who knows if I will be around to advise you on what's right and what's not, but please pick a guy or make decisions say to have a kid when you both want it, don't ruin your life by being with people you don't care for, don't believe everything everyone says to you, make them prove to you what they say is true. Don't ever mix lust or love up, lust can and will deny you the opportunity to love, especially if you produce a child to love. You are not the most important thing in your mind, to me you are, but to you, everyone else is. Don't be selfish, learn to give and not just take, giving will make you smile and will allow you to appreciate the fine things in life. Do what you enjoy, try and make a living out of what you enjoy, then you will wake up every morning with a spring in your step and with an ambition to fulfil the day. The children of this world are our future, never ever forget that, what we teach them now is what they will practise, what we do is what they will follow. Never follow a trend, be the trend, make sure the trend you are is a trend people will admire. Family always knows best, listen to advice, even if it's going to hurt you, only family and the people who love you will say the things that you don't want to hear. Deep down you always know when something you do is wrong, make sure you listen to that feeling before it's too late. Money is not everything in life; it will never truly make you happy, don't follow money, follow the true smiles that make you smile.

THE ONLY FEAR I HAVE, IS LEAVING YOU TO BATTLE THIS WORLD ALONE

I know I keep saying this, but please never ever hate me for writing you this book; you can't believe how painful writing this book has been, it's brought me to tears, and emotions I wish to forget but I know they will always remain inside of me. I now know I need to sell the home I brought for you to give your mum the money she desperately wants so I can get her out my life. I know in doing this I will lose seeing you every day, I will forever blame myself, the self blaming will be every single day of my life when I know I can't be with you or see you, even though I know it was never my fault. I will see that it was me that made the final decision to sell the house, that will be the decision that could be the start of our bond breaking, but I'm going crazy having to come home and locking myself in my room with most nights having you following me in to my room so we don't have to confront your mum. I've had enough just as I write this statement being told by your mum that your cousin, my brother's son has scratched your nose today, apparently you told her that he did, when you were both playing. But the truth is that you did that in your sleep the night before because you was sweating, you had the cut in the morning, but your mum who thinks that she knows best says you didn't, what annoys me more is that she calls my nephew, your cousin a loser, a low life because that's the sort of kid he is. Mark my word, I had a go at your mum, because I've had enough of all this abuse all the time, but what hurts more is that my nephew sees you as a sister he doesn't have and may never have, I see the love he has for you, and he would never hurt you, my little nephew follows you around to make sure you don't fall when you run, what a low life kid that is? I'm being sarcastic if you didn't realise, my nephew, your cousin, believe me and I'm sure in time will realise loves you loads, there's times as you both go to the same primary school, he looks out to see you when he's on lunch just to make sure you are ok, but because your mum doesn't see this, she will make up stories in her head she will see people as and how she feels fit to see them as. These are the only stories that she will believe, no matter what I or anyone will say to show she is wrong.

MY NEPHEW SEE'S YOU AS A SISTER HE MAY NEVER HAVE

The times that occur when I have a go at your mum which make me shout at your mum really annoy me. I hate doing it, especially when you are in the presence to see me doing it. You have to believe me when I say I do this very little, there are also many occasions that I could rise and do it often, near enough every day I could, but in time I've learnt just to ignore your mum and not talk to her anymore as I've noticed she is my downfall in more ways than one, but when I do it, I look at you and wish I never. I can't believe one person gets my emotions so wound up; it makes me react to the extent that I have no option but to shout, she really knows how to push me to my limit and beyond. Your mum does tell me when I begin the shouting that I shouldn't because of you, and I know she makes me shout on purpose, she gets a thrill out of my reactions towards her, but the thing that annoys me is that I'm only reacting because she really is not putting you first or she is being bang out of order towards me. At the point when I'm shouting I'm just too wound up to even notice what I am doing or what is around me, but when I do calm down, I always see you run to me and jump in my arms and give me a cuddle, your mum say's I scare you, but if I did scare you then surly you wouldn't want me, instead I personally believe you feel my pain, you feel how sad I am and maybe you feel how upset your mum makes me. Maybe that's why you come to comfort me the way you do, because maybe you have learnt through the way I have brought you up, and the way I show you attention when you are down, maybe it's your way of comforting me when I am sad, because to see the one thing you love and care for hurt and sad, you would do anything for them. I've never actually thought about this until now as I've wrote it, it actually makes sense, you must hate seeing me upset now days, which is why even when I am sad and I don't feel I show it on the outside, I somehow always get a hug and kiss from you, I believe you know when I am down and hurt and you may not be able to show it that you know I am, but I must mean so much to you if you can instantly tell.

As I said I hate shouting the way I do, because you shouldn't experience what you do, but how much longer can I just accept what I am experiencing, how much longer can I continue without any sort of reaction that will one day seriously get me into trouble.

MAYBE ANOTHER REASON TO WHY I WANT TO SHARE MY STORY

Maybe that's another reason to my thinking of writing this book, maybe it's like a diary of things I've had to deal with, to show the world people like me need support from the government or the law, because if I do react I would be the one who gets in trouble, and the cause would get away with it as if they were innocent. At work when things go wrong, we have to drill down to the root cause so we can correct the issue so it does not happen again. Surly that sort of thinking should apply to what I am dealing with here, especially in regards to your mum. I know if I said a word to the authorities I'd be looked at as if I was mad, but if your mum said a word or even lied about me to any authorities then they would come down on me like a ton of bricks, maybe that's the other reason, I want fathers to be seen as an equal parent to a child because to a child that's the most important factor in all this, the child's best interest. Hopefully my story can and will help your cause and many other children's cause's that need a reality check in this world, a world that we all live in. Give fathers respect and look at the root cause to why a child has to suffer with the heart ache of a broken family, but please understand I know there are many mothers that also deserve the respect, so please don't think I am just singing one tune and ignoring the mothers, respect should be given to both sets of parents, but ultimately the child in the centre of all this saga is the priority.

LET'S LOOK AT THE ROOT CAUSE

Seriously when's this story ever going to end, I have tried to bring this story to an end on numerous occasions now, but I am unable to as things just keep happening. How much more abuse can I take from your mum slagging off my family, just like when your mum constantly slagged off your nene, saying she is a witch, telling me she didn't know how to bring up children, calling her a foreigner who couldn't speak English. You're mum needs to appreciate people, and stop loving herself, she needs to look in the mirror and see who can't look after children. It's not just my mum your mum slag's off, in fact I don't think there's one family member of mine she hasn't, the one that got me fuming was on a night that I had my managers Christmas party, we had arranged to do it in January due to the fact that December is a very busy period for us in our stores and unable to take an evening out of our schedule. I had told her in advance that I was going to go out for a meal that evening and that she would have to look after you day and night, that Saturday I get a phone call telling me that she is going out and I must find someone to have you if I wanted to go out. Your nene will have you on short notice, she will cancel all her plans to have you, but luckily that evening your hala, my niece and nephew had come down to stay at your uncles house. Your hala pleaded with me to have you once she found out about the circumstance. I agreed and I asked your mum to drop you off at uncle's house which is what she did. This is when my niece saw what was happening, not knowing the whole story of what I've explained but knew that she didn't show affection as a mum like her should. My niece is similar to your mum in a way that she likes to get attention from an audience, especially through social media, and she left a status on her facebook saying how some mothers didn't deserve to have children, and that they shouldn't push aside their children as and when it suits them. You need to understand this status never included a name, although it may have been aimed towards your mum, it was never associated with your mum's name, and so no one inside my niece's circle of friends would ever have known it was about your mum as they wouldn't even know who she is. That status however rang alarm bells as your mum and my niece were still friends with each other for whatever reason. Your mum first text me telling me to get her to delete it, then phoning me telling me that my niece was this and that, and I won't write what she said because it will cause more arguments than it's worth towards your mum, but it made me angry and I gave your mum an ear full telling her to stop getting me involved in protecting her over my family.

I'VE HAD ENOUGH OF PROTECTING AND DEFENDING YOUR MUM OVER MY FAMILY

I told my niece to delete and she did, I told your mum it was deleted because I felt it was wrong and not because it was for your mum's sake. I also told your mum to stop slagging her off or I would make things worse, she stopped, she even apologised for it, but this is your mum, people can see on the outside world what she is like, although she does put on a good show for her own friends and family to fool them but in her world, in her own thoughts, she's the best person, and how dare someone say she's not, god knows what she'll think about this book when she reads it? But then again I actually don't think she will; I believe your mum will stay clear from it, as your mum always hides from the truth.

An even funnier thing is that she even used to slag off my families religion which is Muslim, I may add I don't practise this myself as I have no belief in to any religion whatsoever. She used to slag off the religion calling us terrorists saying how stupid it was, but I was ignorant, I ignored her, I actually didn't take notice of her, but how ironic is it now, that since she started going out with an Egyptian guy, she has started converting to a Muslim. I only found this out by accident, your mum kept taking your hair dryer because she broke her one, I went into her walk in closet to get it back one morning as I bathed you and your mum was at work. When I looked up I found a book on the shelf just looking at me, then as I looked on I found more books, the books included how to pray, the Quran, the Muslim woman's handbook, a pray mat, the holy Quran, the Muslim marriage guide, as well as photos of this guy, who may I add looks older than me. On one particular photo it seems both your mum and him look out of it as they both smoked. I can't explain how stressed and worried I began to get with all this, in the back of my head with your mum stealing your passport, and with my friend bringing to my attention that your mums twitter stated that she was Egypt bound, I have no idea what your mum was up to. I told your hala she told me to go to the police, but I never because I just can't get it into my head that she would ever take you away from me, she doesn't spend time with you now, why would she want you full time, but what annoys me more is that when I question your mum she never tells me the truth, tells me that it was an old status on her twitter she tells me I'm crazy for thinking she is converting and that she would never take you to Egypt because there's no future for you out there, but what will stop her once I sell up and move out this house and give her money.

WHAT AM I MEANT TO THINK?

Back to my family, we are a family who looks after you the right way; I believe your mum does slag off my family to maybe take me over my breaking point, but also because she wants to prove to herself maybe that she is a good mother, and I honestly do wish that one day she can be the mother you deserve.

I'm proud of you, and I love to boast about you on my facebook to all my friends and family, by posting pictures of you, I've done this even when I was with your mum. I posted pictures of us all, but since our breakdown I've taken family pictures off and de-tagged your mum from as many pictures as possible, but obviously some pictures of you remain with your mum having her name tagged and connected too. After all she's you're mum, and I have to live with that. Now what I don't expect is that I have random guys with Muslim names, as they have Arabic symbols based as their name liking pictures of you on your own. First things first these guys to me are unknown, secondly they aren't family, and to me this is what you call paedophilic and I said this to your mum, her response was simple, and may I add as she responded to me with her answer she was smiling like she won a gold medal at the Olympics. I was told its not her fault that everyone loves her, I couldn't believe what I was hearing, I just told her if this kept happening I would report it to the police as its sick. Personally I couldn't believe your mum, it's all to do with ego, attention and being better than everyone else, maybe she was taking a dig at me, maybe she was trying to be competitive with me towards how many people I had chasing me, but as I explained it's no contest, and I only want one decent girl, not many inappropriate, not nice, potential partners, but again actions speak louder than words and her actions showed its all self centred needs.

I'VE BITTEN MY TONGUE ON FAR TOO MANY OCCASIONS

I got very close to going to the police once because your mum started accusing me whilst I was putting you to bed, she was out and about as always, probably high on her head, apparently I had posted a sex video of me and her from when we first got together. She threatened me that she was going to get me arrested, threatened me that I was going to lose everything. I promise you I never have, in fact this video was on a very old phone of mine, and the truth of the matter is that this phone is a phone I gave to your mum when your mum's phone broke. I never had any other footage of this after that day which was probably a couple of months after that footage was taken. I know you don't need to know what me and your mum got up to, to be honest I don't really want to remember but it's all a realisation to you, to understand what I have had to deal with and what I have to take. That evening I can't explain how angry and frustrated I felt again, my head began spinning, my heart was racing and I should be grateful your mum wasn't around to accuse me to my face or I think that would have made me hit her. To me she probably lost the phone, or even gave the phone to a friend and it's them that posted the video online. At that moment I was angry, I phoned your hala asked what to do, she told me to go to the police, because she was now taking things too far with all these accusations.

I took you out of bed, as much as I didn't want to because you was tired, your mum wasn't answering any of my phone calls or replying to my text messages, I only had one option and that was to go to the police, I put you in the car, I was taking you to uncle's house to put you to bed there and then I was to go to the police station. It was at this moment I thought I'd pop into your nanny's house to spill the beans on your mum converting to a Muslim because your mum was playing to many mind games with me and I thought about being a parent and thought if you were doing something wrong that I would want to know. Your nanny wasn't in, but your grandpa was, I told him about the sex video, he kind of backed me up, but I knew where his loyalties laid, exactly the same where mine would, with my daughter. I then told him about your mum converting to a Muslim, showed him the photos of the books I found, he looked sick to see them, he phoned your nanny in front of me, said to her, "we have a big problem, she's converting" the funny thing is, your nanny knew about the conversion, but your grandpa didn't.

I actually lost more respect for your nanny at that moment, how can you keep something like this away from her daughters father, and this to me is the mentality that maybe a lot of the world don't understand. A father has and should know everything about their children. It's this sort of mentality where you keep secrets from fathers that cause problems in society because mothers feel they have more power than the father. I felt sorry for your grandpa, I could see a lot of your mum in your nanny, all lies and secrets and maybe always about her. I'm not sure if this was a good thing, a bad thing or a lucky thing for your mum, but on my travels to our uncles house to drop you off your mum phoned me up, telling me she had made a mistake, and it couldn't be me that posted the video, why did I turn back? Why did I not just go to the police? Every accusation or everything your mum does takes me to another level of frustration, I never want to hurt or get your mum in trouble, but I believe she will one day, but how much more can I take? Not as a father, but as a human being, how much can one individual take before crumbling to a point of no return?

I AM VERY CLOSE TO LOSING THE PLOT, VERY CLOSE TO CRUMBLING AWAY

If I do crumble, and I do something wrong, the authorities will come down on me so hard, but as I said surely they should look at the root cause, but we all know they wouldn't. How much more can I do to reassure you? Reassurance though is something I just can't do anymore, as I come to the near completion of this book, you have started asking me a specific question, a question in which I just reply with I don't know. You keep asking me why mummy doesn't play with you, but I don't reassure you anymore with your mum's best interest, as I said I tell you I don't know why she doesn't, but I reassure you that daddy will play with you all the time. The thing that puzzles me with all this, is the reality in to your mum's thoughts, your mum always said I wasn't around for her as I was busy at work making money for her and building a home and future for you both, she admits that she looked elsewhere for attention, very similar if you ask me to what she is doing with you. I believe you have got to the stage where you understand, you notice your mum doesn't play with you, and you're now voicing your views or maybe concerns to people you trust which is normally me, nene, auntie or uncle. Your mum should realise that just like her, although you're mum was an adult and should have known better and should have understood that I was working hard for her and what she wanted.

Your mum should ultimately know if you don't get attention from her, you will look elsewhere for this attention, maybe it's too late for your mum, but your mum needs to realise I'm not backing down as a father to my child, and I'm not going to turn my back from you anymore. If you call for me, your mum is literally going to have to pull you off me, because I've had enough of your mum, in particular for when it suits her to be a mum, and have mum time with you, which is never anymore than an hour. Examples are like when she comes half way through me giving you your bath, or when I'm putting you to sleep just to take you away because maybe she is now ready to be a mum because maybe her programme is finished or none of her boyfriends want to chat. On all occasions you scream the house down, but what she and no one else realises is that you ask me later or the next day, why I didn't bath you and why I let mummy bath you, a reply which is the only reply I can give which is mummy has to, to which I get the reply, but I want you. Tell me how I am meant to cope with all this? Tell me what I can do which won't start a fight, because if it does then you will again witness an environment I don't wish you to see, if I do react to what she does, I will always be seen as the bad guy, so tell me what options I have that I can do away from being silent?

MUMMY REALLY DOES HAVE TO SPEND TIME WITH YOU

Yes I know this story will never end, but your mum is making a drama out of this now, seriously the things she does to me, the way she acts are things, are stories that are seen in made up storylines in soaps on TV. August 2014, I told your mum a week prior that I needed her to pick you up on a Tuesday evening as I was due to work late, on the morning of the Tuesday I reminded her as I was walking out the house with you, asking her what time she was going to pick you up. Your mum forgot, in fact I got the blame for not reminding her the day before. I asked why she couldn't pick you up, her answer, or shall I say her reply was that she didn't have her car as she car shares into work. My reply if I dare spoke out would and should have been, whose more important, your daughter or car share, phone whoever your car sharing with and tell them your daughter needs you to pick her up, or tell them in the afternoon that you had to re-route on the way home to go get your daughter. Why she couldn't pick you up is another reason to me that winds me up, it's the luxury your mum wants in life of having things her way when she wants it, having a kid is just an obstacle in her life, she only wants a daughter when it suits her, and she will never ever put herself out for her daughter. I'm to date still waiting for her to do this, instead when she told me she couldn't pick you up, my exact words were, don't worry I'll get my mum to have her over night, I'm so grateful for your nene, without her, I would have been lost.

WORDS CAN'T DESCRIBE HOW GRATEFUL I AM FOR YOUR NENE

That exact day whilst I was at work, I was fuming inside as I thought about your mum not picking you up, and not changing her plans, it was at this point I thought the time was right to tell her I wanted to sell, bear in mind I always had intentions of selling up on completion of this book, because I would have a clear view of my life, but the anger I had was taking over my thoughts so I text her, I text because I can't talk to your mum anymore, I can't even sit or stay in the room with such a childish adult, I told her I had to sell up, her exact words were that she wants thirty grand now, not twenty grand. Apparently she needs to set up a new life, when in my eyes she destroyed the one she had, apparently she had my kid and that's what it's worth to be free or she'll just sit in the house doing what she is doing and not paying no bills and eating my food. Tell me what I have to do to get rid of her, I have no fight to take this to court, as I said I'd rather the whole world reads my story, to judge your mum and talk about her behind her back. I deserve my life back, and I think it's a price I have to pay for you and me.

With the fear that will never fade from my thoughts that she will take you away from me, although your mum keeps telling me I'm paranoid, but every time in the past she told me that, I was proven to be right with my gut feelings. I won't trust your mum ever, and I promise if she ever takes you away from me without me knowing, especially to another country then I promise you that I will hunt her down. I don't care what law or what authorities read this part of my book, all I ask is for any decent parent who loves their child the way I do, and does everything they possibly can for them every day of their life, then I ask them to be honest with what they would do. This is what annoys me with the world we live in, we hide away from the truth because sometimes the truth can hurt and people are unsure of what to think about it. If what I am about to write and what you are about to read is wrong, then maybe my mental state is not right, but I know I will always do what is right for you, and having you taken away from me, when you want me is firstly out of order on you, and secondly out of order on me, because you're not just taking you away from me, I'm being taken away from you.

So I will hunt your mum down, I will take you back, and probably with the state of mind I would be in, I would kill your mum with my two bare hands, I know many people will think I'm being harsh right now, and out of order for saying this, but I am not scared of saying the truth I'm not going to dress things up to make me look like a saint, any parent who loves and wants to protect their child, where their child only feels safe and wants them will understand what I am trying to say, you belong to me, and you will be with me because that is what you want. I told you're mum that I would have you weekdays and she could have you weekends or just Friday nights and Saturdays, your mum's response was simple that she wants to see you, well in my eyes your mum is also eyeing up the benefits that come along from having a child, I beg the authorities if they read this, to reconsider the application and I also plead with the authorities to help me have you majority of the time, after all I've brought you up with nene, but most importantly it's obvious you want me and no one else. But give me credit, I still know you have to see your mum, I know for you to live as normal a life as you can, you need both of us around.

TWENTY-FIFTH AUGUST 2014

If you think your mum will change in time, any hope that I hold within myself that maybe that will happen has probably gone as I seriously now come to an end of writing this story. As I write this part of the story the date is the twenty-fifth of August 2014. It's near nine in the evening and the house is quite, you're asleep in my bed, snoring away, I'm sitting upon my bed with my laptop writing away, and your mum is away in your room, probably sleeping. You're mum went to Egypt over a week ago, she returned back at just gone three in the morning and I am shocked to what she has done today.

Your mum phoned you on her birthday, and then on two other occasions, I applaud her for that. Luckily for me, I've been on holiday from work, I took two weeks off from being tired, and in need of a good rest, but also because it's time I got this house ready to sell. You and I went away to great Yarmouth with your hala, your two cousins and nene for five days, if I'm honest it was really nice to get away from this house, the same scenery, the same issues and was a real eye opener for me because for the first time you was born I didn't have your mum around, there was no work, it was just me and you. This holiday proved to me that I work too hard, and I need to stop before it kills me, or ruins us, secondly and most importantly it showed me what a nasty person your mum is, your overall aura, your overall attitude changed, and even your auntie noticed the difference on your return saying you were much happier.

Whilst on holiday I realised in a normal day although I'm there for you I seem to rush being with you, and just taking my time with you has been so precious to me, I think it's made us impossibly even closer. The proof to this is that when I was putting you to bed one evening whilst on holiday, you just gave me a kiss and told me you loved me, you laid down to sleep, then sat up again and told me that you loved me lots and lots, your nene heard this, and she had to come in and give you a hug because I think she felt and realised you understand everything I do for you, and I actually believe for maybe the first time your nene realised how close you are to me, and how much you depend on me.

I LOVE YOU LOTS AND LOTS DADDY

On return from holiday it was the time to clean and do minor DIY repairs to the house, and in the two days prior to your mum coming back, I was able to do loads of work inside and outside of the house, even whilst looking after you, the problem for me began on the return of your mum. Firstly I never knew when she was due back, secondly I didn't care if she did or not, but on her return, instantly when I heard the house door open and when I heard the suitcase being struggled up the stairs, a massive part of me sank. I understand why she couldn't come and give you a kiss whilst you slept because you were with me, but what I don't understand is her attitude towards you during her first day back.

Bear in mind your mum has not seen you for over a week, surly a parent would be itching and anticipating for their child to wake to spend time with them, but not your mum. Look, she did call you into your room when she heard you talking to me in the morning, you was shocked to hear her voice, I told you to go and say hello to mummy, you did, fair play to your mum she said she missed you and gave you a kiss, but you came back to me, and as usual I took you downstairs to give you breakfast. The door to your room, the room where your mum was in, was shut as we walked past it to go downstairs, you never shut it, your mum did, I presume sleep was more important.

YOUR MUM DID NOT SEE YOU FOR OVER A WEEK

You got to understand if I didn't see you for a whole week, I'd want you all day to just feel your love but also for you to understand that I was still here for you. I don't know what goes through your mums head, I took you to the supermarket in the morning to get some paint brushes as I wanted to paint the door and a few spots around the house, on our return your mum was seated in her usual spot on the sofa, watching all her TV programmes she had missed whilst away, these had all been pre-recorded, and one by one throughout the day, show after show, reality show after reality show these were all watched.

Now prior to me even knowing that your mum was going to do this, I was talking to you in the car on the way to get the paint brushes and I asked if you would let me paint and you could play with mummy, your answer without hesitation was mummy don't play with me, she watches tele. Wow, even you know this.

Throughout the day I did DIY, I cooked, I cleaned, and I looked after you, I didn't say a word to your mum, I was really annoyed with her, and more than anything disgusted that she showed no love or any emotion to wanting to spend time with you. I even thought she would bath you and put you to bed considering she hasn't done it for a while, but no, she didn't show any interest. I write this as it has happened today, it's fresh in my memory, and as I hear you breathe in your sleep, I can't understand how a parent can do this to their child, I can't believe the mother of my child is like this to my child.

I now know why I am like I am to you, I am the man, a dad who is doing everything I can to possibly fill the void you may have of a mother, and believe me I am doing such a good job and I don't need anyone to tell me this. Tonight you fell asleep cuddled up to me in bed whilst we watched Wall-e, you're so clever, you understand every emotion that little robot has without any words, as you tell me when he is sad, or happy. Again if you can see this in an animated robot, I'm sure you understand every little bit of neglect that happens to you by a human being.

AT SUCH A YOUNG TENDER AGE, YOU UNDERSTAND SO MUCH

During the day there was two instances, you were playing in your sand box I built you, you got sand in your eye, your mum was the closest to you as I was painting the ceiling in the hall way, you cried out for me, I heard your mum saying I'm here, and I even think she held you because your cry for me just got louder but you came running round the corner into my arms. Just like when I cooked you dinner and you was eating a carrot, again your mum was the closest as you bit your tongue, your mum tried to comfort you, but again came running to me for a hug, and asking me to feed you, to which I said yes, to which your mum walked upstairs as I sat you on my knee, and read you a story as I fed you.

I think your mum is getting the point, but she won't accept it, I do believe there is a lot of pressure from your nanny towards your mum in regards to you, I am one hundred percent sure that your nanny is unaware of the lack and lazy attitude your mum has towards you away from her presence, but today has just confirmed everything to me, your mum disgusts me for not wanting you, not wanting to spend time with you, it just proves my point that your mum is a trophy mum and in eyes she only wants to be a mum for the wrong reasons.

YOU WERE NEVER A MISTAKE

You have never been a mistake in my life; your mum as I've said has made being a dad to you extremely difficult. It be crazy if I didn't admit if I had never thought of a life without you, without your mum. There's times I think how life would be if I never met your mum, and it's a nice thought, then I think of you. It's strange because if I never met your mum, I would never have met you, you wouldn't even be a thought, so I would never have known who you were, I wouldn't have known then what I would have been missing by not having you, and that sort of life would be nice.

I'm not going to lie to you and say things you want to hear. That sort of life would be peaceful, no stress, no responsibilities, if I didn't like something I'd be able to make a decision and move on to the next or next idea I had, you could say it's a lot like your mum's current life situation, but obviously I'd know how to respect people. Then I ask myself this question, knowing the life I have now, and knowing the life I could have if I didn't meet your mum, which life do I want? It would be nice to have that previous life, but it's better to have you, and that thought will never ever change, I can and am planning to go back to a non stressful life without your mum, I'm hoping to have you and my life back, and then everything will be perfect. So please never stress yourself that you destroyed my life, never fear that I have struggled because of you, never ever worry that I'm tired or stressed or whatever else comes in with parenthood. All I want you to remember is that we all had choices, and we will still have choices in life, I chose to look after you, I chose to get bruised and battered by your mum to look after you the best possible way, I chose to put you ahead of me, and as I said I would do it all over again for you, but as I have explained, this book is to close a chapter of my life with your mum, and help me regain my life which will make my life, but ultimately your life better.

I WANT TO MAKE OUR LIFE BETTER

Your mum does love you in her own funny sort of way; never ever think that she doesn't. Yes your mum and I will never be together although our paths crossed in the past too have you. I know my life would never be complete without you now, and I'm sure your mum feels the same when I say that we are both blessed to have you. As for your mum, I personally from what I see think there is something missing in her thoughts, maybe she needs help but denies it, I did that after all, but I'm a strong character and don't allow others to manipulate my mind, maybe other people have influenced your mum too much.

I believe she needs to accept her mistakes and stop making mistakes to try and cover her mistakes. She needs to realise that she has a beautiful baby girl, I know that day will come, I hope and pray it's not too late when she does, because I know the older you get, the more you grow with your mum just being called a mum and not acting like one will ultimately not be enough. Maybe its hearing what she has done, maybe through reading this book to actually realise what she has done, and what she has lost. Maybe she now needs to grieve because my grieving has been done. I'm now ready to move on with my life.

Just remember daddy will always be there for you, no matter where we may be or when it may be, although I may not always be there by your side, I promise I will always be watching, and I will be forever protecting you. This is a motto which I have now got a tattoo of on the inside of my lower left arm by my wrist. I've always been against tattoos saying if you get one, it must mean something, there is nothing in the world that means more to me and nothing ever will, your love will be in me forever, so this motto has now scar'd my body, because this story has scar'd me for the rest of my life. The tears you see in the eyes of my tattoo are the tears I cry for you when I am not near you, but fear not, I'm "always watching, forever protecting"

It was strange reaction from you when I actually got this tattoo because when you saw it for the first time, you actually got scared, and just cuddled me and didn't want to let go of me. In time you started asking me questions, asking why the eyes were crying and whose eyes they were. When you finally realised they were my eyes and it was my tears when I missed you, I think you realised how sad I am when I am away from you, maybe it was reassurance that you may have needed to let you know that I don't want to push you away.

ALWAYS WATCHING, FOREVER PROTECTING

I now begin to write my last paragraph or section of this story, it's a paragraph or a section that proves everything we have been through and everything I have spoke about has been worthwhile. Without you, I would never know what love was, without you I wouldn't have realised how important it is not to focus on your own self, but most importantly it's allowed me to show someone how to care and grow by learning and living by being in my eyes a perfect role model, my reward for all this is the love you show me at all times.

I've been in tears since nine o'clock Thursday the fourth of September 2014. No one knows the tears I'm shedding, as they are tears I don't want anyone to see and are tears that flood my eyes when no one is around. I said goodbye to you on that morning as you were going on holiday with your mum, nanny and your mum's cousin. I can't get out my head my last cuddle with you, I can't get out my head you waving at me as I drove off as I couldn't bear to hang around to see you and everyone drive off with suitcases, I just had to get out before anyone could see me cry. I apologise in advance if what I write now is very emotional but I'm writing exactly how I feel right this second because I miss you so much, and me writing is the only thing I can do to let it out my system, I have no one to talk to.

I drove to your school as I had to hand over a sheet to confirm you would not be attending school for a week, why your mum didn't do it when she is the one taking you away is again an annoying trait your mum has, she never does anything that won't influence herself. Believe me this is going to be the longest week I have ever known, this is going to be the longest I have been apart from you, and I know it's going to kill me inside. People just don't understand the pain or torture I am going through. They all tell me it will do me good to be away from you, it will do us good to be apart, these are the comments from people who will never know the truth of how we are, they are the ones who don't know how reliant you are to me, they are the ones who don't hear you cry for daddy at every occasion. This is the point I am trying to make, no one understands and I am beginning to think that no one ever will. I just wish someone would come to me and give me a hug and tell me they understand the pain and heartache I am going through, because I really do feel that I am in this on my own and the more I think like this, the more it effects my thoughts.

I JUST WANT A HUG AND FOR SOMEONE TO UNDERSTAND

I knew I would struggle this is why the day before you left I brought you this teddy that turns into a pillow, I actually brought two, one for both of us. The evening before you left I gave it to you and I told you that no matter how much you missed me, and no matter how much you would call for me, because I know you will, as that's all that echo's in my ears. I told you when you feel like this to cuddle the teddy and give it a kiss and that I would do the same with my teddy as I wouldn't be able to come to your aid. I also told you to sleep on your pillow and daddy would always be with you giving you cuddles and making sure you sleep well.

That morning all I did was cry as I went to your school it took me half hour just to get out the car to go to the schools reception. I just handed the form in and left, as I entered my car I just continued to cry, I couldn't take this anymore, my chest was now hurting, my eyes were hurting, I was driving myself mad with all this thinking, so I just drove to the doctors. It was just an instinct I did, no actual thought about why I wanted to see a doctor, but I had no one else to go to.

I went to the reception desk and asked to book an appointment, they asked if it was an emergency, I said no, maybe I should have said yes. The lady at the desk told me they were fully booked, even on my next day off they had nothing available, I told them I would be back in contact and left. I'm too scared to ask for help, in saying that do I really think I'm ill or need help? No I don't, well maybe I do, but all that I do know is that I can't keep living this way. All I know is that I just want you back, I just want to know your safe and I want a hug and a kiss, no doctor in this world can make a broken heart better.

No DOCTOR CAN FIX A BROKEN HEART

During the week where you was going to be away from me, I was suppose to stay with your nene, but after feeling the way I did, and being all emotional, I made the decision to lock myself in this house when not at work so I could let my tears naturally flow. Maybe that was the wrong thing to do, but it's the only thing I could do as I would feel uncomfortable being all emotional in front of my family and pretending I was fine.

The more I think about what has happened to me since you were born, the more it doesn't make sense. Your mum can afford to take you abroad because she has no commitments or responsibilities; I can't afford to do that for you because I put a house over your head and buy you all the essential things you need as a child growing up from the moment you were born. Yes we went away to great Yarmouth, but it's nothing special, and most of that was thanks to your hala. I hope one day you realise that trophy moments mean nothing in life, it's the moments that we have shared that are the most important, and I hope you take this as a learning and live your life this way.

This heartache I feel is because you're all I know, you're all I've focused on since you were born, and because of this I have forgot about everything else, in fact I know of nothing else. I've never taken you away from your mum, even when we went great Yarmouth it was during the week your mum went Egypt. Your mum broke your family and ultimately took me away from you, she has now taken you to another country which means you're away from me, and to me that is the hardest thing to deal with because I have no idea where you are, I have no idea how you are and I can't hear you or see you to protect you.

THIS IS WHAT THE STORY WAS ALL ABOUT

This is what this story is all about, it's about me bringing you up, me looking out for you with what I see best, making sure your never hurt and it's all about us. Without you I am lost, without you I don't know what to do with my spare time. I actually don't have anyone worthy to spend my time with, so no wonder my tears fall from the eyes upon my face when I'm not with you, and this is why it's going to take someone special to win me.

I've spoke to you a few times whilst you were away, but that just makes it worse for me, makes me miss you even more then I actually do. I just can't wait to see you when you get back; I'm going to hug you like you have never been hugged before.

And that's what I did, you got the biggest hug, and for me the best thing was, I heard your mums car pull up outside the house, I deliberately left my window open so If I did fall asleep I could hear any sort of noise to wake me up as you were coming back in the late hours of the night. I heard you call "daddy, where's daddy" and that was it, my eyes opened, you came upstairs and gave me that hug, and you cuddled up next to me still holding your teddy that I got you. I doubt anyone in the world will understand how I feel? I doubt they will understand one hundred percent everything I say in this book? But to know you missed me and your first thought was me, just means the world to me, it makes everything I have ever done, every sacrifice in my life for you has been worth it.

YOUR FIRST THOUGHT WAS ME, WHICH MEANS THE WORLD TO ME

But your mum's mind games started again on her and your return from holiday, she told me she had resigned from her job as they did not allow her the time off to go on holiday with you. Again how would she of not known her holiday had not been authorised prior to her going? You see your mum knew for about six months you were going away, surely she got this date authorised by her work place, even your mum couldn't be that stupid to only tell them last minute she was going?

But my mind started working overtime again, thinking I had recently told your mum I want to sell the house, what was she up to? Did she now want to be a full time mum, did she want the benefits that much she would do anything for them, I could only see one picture in all of this, all I could see was that she was a mum, and that she would take you away from me just so she could gain all the benefits of a single mum. As I said my mind started working overtime and my first instinct was that I would resign to, and we will see who you want to be with, as I said I am not ready and never will be ready to be a part time dad, especially when I've been full time with you from the day you were born.

YOUR MUM JUST GOT UP AND LEFT, AGAIN

But then one day your mum disappeared, I got a call to say she was going away for a bit, and this is after I told her as she weren't working I would do a few late nights and she would have to pick you up from school or from nene, she agreed but went against what she agreed, this not only left me but also you in limbo. Again, you would have thought that her not having to work she would spend the time with you, she would take you to school and pick you up, but you would think wrong. Your mum for the first two days did this, but after this would not want to take you, I didn't ask why? But it was obvious your mum didn't want to wake up early to look after you, I have no proof of this but tell me why she wouldn't acknowledge you in the morning's, would make sure her door was shut to where she was sleeping, so again it was still up to me to take you to nene even though she was doing nothing all day, nene would take you to school and then for your mum to pick you up. Yet again that got me thinking, because you would fall asleep in the car on the way home, and your mum would just put you to bed, so tell me how much time did she actually spend with you?

So where did your mum go, I personally believe she went Egypt again, your mum is so secretive that even if I asked she would lie. What was even stranger is that your nanny phoned me up asking me where your mum was after a couple of days of her being absent all because she couldn't get hold of your mum and must have been worried. I told her she just left and probably went Egypt, your nanny's response was that she never went Egypt without saying anything before, which proves to me your mum does go there and it also proves to me that your mum is up to something that she doesn't want people to know about, especially if she can't tell her own mum.

Now I have no evidence but did your mum resign? Or did she get dismissed or asked to leave? Why did your mum make the decision to leave work? Was it for the reason she gave? Or is it for a reason I think of, that would make more sense. I believe the holiday your mum went with you was always authorised, however your mum asked for more time off to go Egypt on her return from the holiday with you, but with the amount of time your mum has taken off it is clear and acceptable for her work place to say no, she must have run out of allowance. To me this is why she resigned, that to me makes more sense, bear in mind I deal with incidents with punctuality and absence in my own job so I know all the legislations and what you can and can't do. So yet again, your mum wanted her boyfriend in her spare time, and you were pushed aside to be with me.

You're mum will never have the right to question me as a father, because I have always put you first, never ever pushed you aside for my needs.

NO ONE WILL EVER HAVE THE RIGHT TO QUESTION ME, WHICH INCLUDES YOUR MUM

As silly as this may sound, with everything that has happened to me, and the way my mind seems to work these days, I just don't feel I am allowed to be happy. How can I smile? How can I laugh? Or even have any fun? If inside me all that I feel is sadness. Don't get me wrong, I'm not like this all the time, it's only when I am away from you that I feel like this, I somewhat feel guilty that I am not allowed to be happy away from you. There have been occasions where I sometimes smile, then I think of you and I walk away from what made me smile. I'm trying to sum it up to you just how or why I feel like this and I can't find the words to express my feelings, maybe the only way I can tell you is that my smiles, my laughter and my fun side is only for you, because you're the only one in this cruel world that deserves the best of me. Maybe that's why I hate this world, because I don't understand it, smiles and laughter should be hidden for others, with you there not fake, that's why they shine with glory when I am with you.

When you get older and you read this story, I just want one thing from you, I don't want you to say a word, I don't want you to bring any of this pain back in to my mind, I just want you to come over to me, and give me a hug, that's all I want, that hug will tell me everything I need to know, that hug will speak a thousand words.

This is the end of my story, for now I will close this chapter and begin my fight for our freedom. I'm determined to make sure you're unaffected in all this, and I hope I survive the battle, as I said I have no fight left, and if your mum continues her games I have no idea what will happen, as I've said there is only so much a human being can take, and I've exhausted that a very long time ago so I have no idea how I could possibly react to anything she does anymore.

THANK YOU

Just to summarise where I am in my life as I've come to the end of this story. I also want to take this opportunity to personally say thank you to an amazing girl who I work with who I trusted to read my book to help me correct some spellings and possible grammar mistakes. She is the sole person who realised I needed help prior to reading any of this book; she is the only one who has ever asked if I needed help and recommended how to get help, and it's because of her friendship and care towards me that I finally went to a doctor. The girl I work with understood me and that's all I ever asked for, she didn't judge who I was even after hearing all the rumours about my past through work colleagues, she realised my smiles were not real and asked to read my book as she was aware of my writing. Maybe she read the book at the right time as she herself was going through some things in her life at that particular moment. Pleasing for me was that she could relate to everything I had wrote through her own life experiences. I don't have any friends or family who were that brave or honest to confront me about getting help, even those that saw me deteriorate, so I sincerely thank her, and I wish her all the best in the future, I know why I say that, as she will to, she has a friend for life in me and she needs to be aware of that, I will always be there to help if she ever needs anything and I won't say that to, to many people any more, I know the ones I can trust now days.

I REFUSE TO TAKE ANY MEDICATION

As for the doctor, he couldn't believe it's taken me over two years to seek help medically; I am to stay in frequent contact with him as well as being referred to a councillor. He has prescribed me some tablets but I at the moment will refuse to take these as I am focused on getting through this without. I won't hide from the fact I need help anymore because I know I do, but that doesn't make me a lesser person for admitting I do, the people who have caused me to need help are the ones who should be ashamed, they are the ones who need to hide. But mark my word my baby girl, I will win this battle and I will write a second part to this book for you and everyone else who may be in the same position as me to show the world it can be done, but for me to do this, I need to have your love and that I know will never fade nor will it ever die and with that in mind I will succeed.

Just remember that I will love you forever my baby girl, that is something I will promise forever.

FOR NOW THE STORY ENDS, BUT BELIEVE ME THERE WILL NEVER BE AN END TO THIS STORY.

TORN APART, MY HEART AND MY LIFE,

Written by Shazia.A

When the storm came to pass, the rain and thunder
I stood there, with my heart asunder,
My broken love, like pieces of mirrors
Through it, I watched my tears tranquilly,
Holding the little fingers of my daughter, I intersect the ignition
Each day, the sun rises, each day my twinge amplifies
And now that my love holds no existence
I slipped away those catastrophes with a faux smile across my face,
So as my little Angel sleeps her night peacefully,
And at dawn when she wakes up, she finds a rainbow every time it rains
I amble through, without a pat on my shoulder,
But the innocent eyes of my child,
Allowed me to see a different world,
Yet, sometimes, I am to endure all ruse life menace
At times, I run away, and I still find myself,
In the middle of a wrecked bridge,
I survived the tempest, and now, I see her growing,
Like a stunning rose, my daughter,
Holding her hands, I am now a fighter,
Smiling through this journey,
I am giving her boundless joy,
I'm here to save her from the worlds of ploys,
Forever and ever

Printed in the United States
By Bookmasters